FOUNDATION

Short Stories for
Personal Management

Sunil Thomas, Ph.D.

SUNIPRINT
A Division of Abraham Thomas Foundation

FOUNDATION
Short Stories for
Personal Management

Sunil Thomas, Ph.D.

Copyright © SUNIPRINT
2025

Cover Design: Sunil Thomas

ISBN: 978-1-965451-08-3

SUNIPRINT
A Division of Abraham Thomas Foundation
11 Cambridge Road, Broomall, PA-19008, USA
E-mail: suniprintbooks@gmail.com

PREFACE

Personal management is the ability to complete tasks efficiently while also focusing on long-term self-growth. It is not just about getting things done but about doing them with purpose, strategy, and consistency. Developing strong habits, time management skills, and a disciplined mindset ensures steady progress over the years. Every effort you put into refining your skills and managing your responsibilities effectively helps build a solid foundation for future success.

Just as a building rests securely on its foundation, so too does a human life depend on the strength of its inner base. Our philosophy, values, education, and experiences form the unseen framework that supports who we are. These elements may not always be visible to others, much like the concrete and steel beneath a skyscraper, but they determine whether we stand firm when pressure mounts or collapse when life shakes us. Without strong foundations, even the most impressive outward appearance cannot endure for long.

Every individual, at some point, faces trials that put these foundations to the test. Challenges may come in the form of personal loss, professional setbacks, or moral dilemmas that demand difficult choices. In those moments, superficial charm, wealth, or status provide little protection. Instead, it is the depth of our convictions, the lessons we have absorbed, and the principles we live by that allow us to weather the storms. Just as a tremor reveals the true quality of a structure, hardships reveal the true character of a person.

When our foundations are strong, time itself becomes a proving ground that does not weaken us but refines us. The years may bring change, adversity, or uncertainty, yet those anchored in truth, wisdom, and integrity remain steady. They may bend but do not break, and like well-built towers, they rise tall again after each test. Investing in our inner foundation— through continual learning, reflection, and the practice of values—ensures that we are prepared not just to survive, but to endure and inspire others along the way.

This book, *Foundation*, is a collection of 100 short stories centered on the theme of personal management. Each story provides insights, lessons, and reflections on how to navigate responsibilities, develop resilience, and maintain discipline in everyday life. Through these narratives, readers will discover how seemingly small tasks and decisions contribute to a larger picture of growth and efficiency.

Whether you are a student, a professional, or someone striving for self-improvement,

Foundation offers valuable perspectives on how to manage life's challenges and opportunities. The stories serve as reminders that the strength of your foundation determines the durability of your journey and the height to which you can rise.

TABLE OF CONTENTS

8

1. THE ROAD PASSING BY

The road that winds past your house is more than just a path of asphalt and gravel—it is a silent witness to the countless lives that have journeyed along it through the years. For generations, people have traveled that road, each carrying their own hopes, burdens, and dreams. Some were travelers searching for opportunity, others were residents stepping out to meet the world. Though we may never know their names or stories, we can imagine the many lives that intersected with that road, leaving behind unseen footprints and echoes of their passage.

Each of those travelers, like us, faced their own share of struggles. Whether it was hardship caused by war, poverty, loss, or personal failure, life inevitably brought them challenges. And yet, they moved forward. We can presume that many of them met adversity with quiet dignity, with resilience, and with a determination to carry on. The road itself, unchanged in its form yet shaped by time, stands as a symbol of persistence through life's trials.

In our lives today, we too face obstacles— emotional struggles, career setbacks, family pressures, and uncertainties about the future. Sometimes these hardships feel isolating, as if no one else could understand what we're going through. But the truth is, the challenges we encounter are rarely unique. Somewhere, sometime, someone else has stood in a similar place, grappling with similar fears and questions. This realization can offer us comfort and perspective.

By remembering the generations who traveled before us, we can draw strength from their example. They endured, and so can we. The road outside our window serves not just as a physical connection between places, but as a metaphorical reminder that life is a journey shared across time. We are part of a continuum, connected by the human experience of struggle and the will to persevere. Just as they did, we too must walk forward with grace and courage, knowing we are not alone.

2. DO NOT DIG DEEPER WHEN YOU ARE IN A HOLE

Shawn had built a thriving business from the ground up, earning a reputation as a successful and driven entrepreneur. For years, his company flourished, providing stable employment to many and securing his place in the community as a respected business leader. However, when a severe economic recession hit, his business took a devastating blow. Revenue plummeted, clients pulled out, and operational costs became unsustainable. One by one, he was forced to let go of employees he had worked with for years—people he considered family.

The emotional toll of these losses, combined with the financial strain, weighed heavily on Shawn. He began to spiral into depression, struggling to cope with the collapse of everything he had worked so hard to build. In an attempt to numb the pain, he turned to alcohol. What started as an occasional drink to take the edge off soon turned into a daily habit of heavy drinking.

Over time, his physical health began to deteriorate alongside his mental well-being. Concerned, he visited his physician, who, after a series of tests, delivered a sobering diagnosis: liver cirrhosis. The years of excessive drinking had taken a serious toll on his body, and now he faced a new, life-threatening challenge.

Life is an unpredictable journey, full of both triumphs and trials. No person—regardless of status, wealth, or strength—has ever walked this Earth without facing some form of adversity. Challenges are an inevitable part of the human experience. They test our resilience, shape our character, and often arrive when we least expect them. While some challenges may seem small and manageable, others can shake the very foundation of our lives.

When difficulties arise, it's natural to feel overwhelmed, frustrated, or even defeated. However, how we respond to those challenges can make all the difference. If we allow ourselves to be consumed by negativity or self-pity, we risk falling deeper into despair. Digging ourselves into a metaphorical hole—by denying reality, avoiding responsibility, or seeking unhealthy coping mechanisms—only worsens the situation. The deeper we dig, the harder it becomes to climb out.

Instead of retreating or giving in to hopelessness, we must strive to face our problems with courage and clarity. Growth often begins in the moments when we choose to rise rather than sink. Challenges, though painful, can be powerful teachers, guiding us toward inner strength and wisdom. It's not about avoiding hardship but learning how to navigate it without losing ourselves in the process.

3. WHEN THE REINS SLIP, HOLD TIGHT

Calvin visited his cousin Felix in the countryside village, a place surrounded by wide open spaces and breathtaking scenery. Upon arrival, he was immediately struck by the vast, sweeping fields that stretched out toward the horizon—so different from the crowded cityscapes he was used to. The clean air and quiet atmosphere brought a sense of peace and excitement. Seeing Calvin's enthusiasm, Felix suggested they fly a kite, taking advantage of the open fields and steady breeze. Calvin's eyes lit up at the idea; it had been years since he last flew a kite, and the thought brought back joyful childhood memories.

As they set up and launched the kite, the wind suddenly turned unpredictable. Gusts came in sharp bursts, tugging the kite wildly in different directions. The kite danced and spun out of control, threatening to crash or break free. Despite the chaos, Calvin never released the string—instead, he gripped it tightly, determined to regain control. His hands strained, but he held firm, refusing to give up. Eventually, the erratic winds began to calm, settling into a gentle, steady breeze. With the tension easing, Calvin was able to guide the kite smoothly through the air. It soared gracefully above the fields, and Calvin, smiling with quiet satisfaction, felt a renewed connection to a simpler joy he had long forgotten.

There are seasons in life when everything feels as if it is slipping through our fingers. Plans collapse, routines break, relations flounder, and we are left with a sense that the world is spinning faster than we can keep up with. In such moments, fear and frustration can cloud our vision, making us believe that control is gone and that we are helpless passengers in our own story. This feeling of being adrift can tempt us to give up on the fight altogether.

Yet, it is precisely in those turbulent times that holding on matters most. The thought of "jumping ship" may feel like the easiest way out, but abandoning your path often means giving up just before the breakthrough arrives. Holding on to the reins does not mean denying the chaos; it means grounding yourself in patience, faith, and resilience. Even when the storm rages, your ability to steer — however slightly — can keep you from being swept away entirely. Each small act of persistence becomes a statement of courage against despair.

In the end, control is not about mastering every detail of life, but about refusing to let challenges dictate your direction. By holding firm to the reins, you remind yourself that you are still the rider, still the decision-maker, even if the terrain is rough. What feels unbearable today can, in time, transform into a lesson, a strength, or a new beginning. The struggle may test you, but it also shapes you — and when the storm settles, you emerge stronger, wiser, and more prepared for the journey ahead.

4. WITH THE HARDEST HIT COMES THE HIGHEST RISE

Kramer returned home exhausted and weighed down by sorrow. His business, which had struggled for quite some time, had finally been taken over by the bank. Despite his relentless effort and countless sleepless nights, he had been unable to turn things around or make a profit. The loss of his livelihood left him feeling defeated, unsure of how to begin again. As he sat in silence, searching for a glimmer of hope, his eyes fell on his young son bouncing a ball. He noticed how, no matter how hard the ball struck the ground, it always rose higher into the air. In that simple moment, Kramer realized that life's hardest blows could be the very force that propels one to greater heights, provided he had the resilience and determination to rise again.

Not long after, his longtime friend Pablo came by to visit. Pablo owned a modest business in another part of the city, but he was preparing to leave for a promising job in a distant land. Rather than selling his business, Pablo offered Kramer a unique opportunity: he could take charge of the business, run it with his full creativity and vision, and in return, share a small portion of the profit with Pablo while keeping the rest. This gesture of trust and generosity filled Kramer with renewed hope. He poured his energy, resourcefulness, and hard-earned lessons into the new venture. Before long, his hard work paid off—the business thrived beyond expectations and grew into a remarkable success, proving that setbacks can often be the beginning of even greater comebacks.

Sometimes in life we face moments when everything seems to slip away—our work, our stability, even our sense of direction. Loss can arrive suddenly or after a long struggle, leaving us with the heavy feeling that all is gone. These experiences test our strength, patience, and faith, often pushing us to the edge of despair. Yet, it is in these very moments of struggle that the seeds of resilience are planted, waiting to be awakened by our will to keep moving forward.

Just as a ball bounces highest when it is struck with the greatest force, life too can propel us upward after the hardest blows. Pain, failure, and disappointment may push us down, but they also give us the opportunity to rise higher than before. Every setback carries within it the possibility of growth, renewal, and a fresh beginning. The challenge lies in how we choose to respond—whether to remain defeated on the ground or to harness the momentum of adversity and rise stronger.

When we embrace this truth, even the darkest times can become stepping stones to a brighter future. Life's hardships are not meant to end our journey but to redirect it, reminding us of our inner strength and untapped potential. By holding onto hope, learning from the past, and applying courage to each new step, we transform difficulties into opportunities. In this way, life becomes not just a story of losses, but a testament to resilience, perseverance, and the ability to rise higher than we ever imagined.

5. STANDING TALL

Rice serves as the staple food for nearly half of the global population, making it one of the most important crops for food security worldwide. Traditionally, rice is cultivated in waterlogged paddies, where controlled flooding supports its growth by suppressing weeds and providing a stable environment. However, excessive or prolonged flooding beyond optimal levels can be detrimental, often causing the plants to die due to oxygen deprivation. Amidst these challenges, the salt- and flood-tolerant rice variety known as *pokkali* stands out as uniquely adapted to thrive under harsh environmental conditions. Originating from coastal regions, pokkali rice has evolved remarkable resilience, enabling it to survive and even flourish in saline, waterlogged soils where conventional rice varieties would fail. Notably, this variety requires no chemical fertilizers or insecticides, making it an environmentally sustainable choice for farmers. One of its most extraordinary traits is its ability to elongate its stems rapidly as floodwaters rise, allowing the plant to grow above the water surface and continue photosynthesis without drowning. This adaptation not only helps *pokkali* withstand severe flooding but also contributes to maintaining yield stability in unpredictable climate scenarios, positioning it as a valuable genetic resource for breeding future resilient rice cultivars amid increasing global climate challenges.

Every human being, no matter their background, will inevitably face adversity at some point in life. Challenges may come in different forms—loss, failure, rejection, or unforeseen hardships—but they are an inseparable part of the human journey. No one is exempt, and it is often through these struggles that people learn resilience, patience, and the true measure of their character. Life was never meant to be a path of constant ease; rather, it is the trials along the way that give depth to our experiences and shape us into who we are meant to become.

When difficulties surround us, it can sometimes feel as though the entire world has collapsed. In such moments, despair may tempt us to give up, but it is precisely then that inner strength must rise. Standing tall does not mean pretending that pain does not exist; it means facing it with courage, refusing to be defined or destroyed by it. Each setback becomes an opportunity to learn, to grow, and to rebuild with even stronger foundations. The act of rising when everything seems to fall apart is a profound declaration that we are more than our circumstances.

Ultimately, adversity teaches us one of life's most important lessons: that true strength is not the absence of fear or suffering but the determination to endure and overcome. Those who stand tall in the face of difficulties often inspire others who are silently battling their own struggles. In standing firm, we prove to ourselves and to the world that no storm lasts forever, and that after darkness, there is always the promise of light. It is this spirit of perseverance that transforms trials into triumphs and leaves behind a legacy of resilience for others to follow.

6. PASSION TRIUMPHS WEALTH

Victor had always nurtured a dream: to own a sprawling electronics store that offered a wide range of products—from audio and video equipment to office supplies, kitchen appliances, and other household devices. Though passionate and determined, Victor's ambition was limited by his modest means. He operated a small electronics shop tucked away near a much larger and more prominent electronic retail outlet. Despite the intimidating competition, Victor remained undeterred.

Every day, he poured his heart into his business. He worked tirelessly to attract customers and build relationships with suppliers. Through persistence and clever negotiation, Victor managed to secure bulk orders from both small enterprises and larger corporations. His dedication began to pay off, and his store gained a loyal customer base. Still, the profits he made, though steady, were not enough to finance the expansion he had always dreamed of.

Then, an unexpected opportunity presented itself. A massive fire broke out at the nearby large electronics store. The damage was extensive, and with the store already struggling financially, the parent company decided to cut its losses and sell the property in its current state. However, due to the ongoing economic recession, there were no interested buyers. The company, eager to offload the damaged asset, turned to Victor as a last resort.

Victor saw more than a burnt building—he saw the chance to turn his lifelong dream into reality. Without wasting time, he approached local banks for financing and reached out to electronic manufacturers he had built rapport with over the years. He presented a bold vision, convincing them of the potential this new store could hold. His determination paid off. With financial backing and supplier support, Victor acquired the property and began transforming it into the large, modern electronics store he had always envisioned.

When the doors finally reopened under Victor's name, customers flocked in—not just for the wide product selection and competitive pricing, but also for the exceptional after-sales service that had become Victor's trademark. His commitment to customer satisfaction set him apart from competitors, and word of mouth quickly spread.

Victor's new store thrived, and what began as a humble operation grew into a well-respected business. His story became an inspiration—a testament to perseverance, smart decision-making, and the power of seizing opportunities when they arise.

Every successful millionaire began their journey with humble beginnings. They didn't start with wealth or fame, but with a spark—an idea, a passion, and a relentless desire to pursue something meaningful. Whether it was launching a small business, inventing a product, or offering a unique service, these individuals poured their time, energy, and heart into their work. They understood that success doesn't happen overnight; it's built day by day, through hard work, learning, and perseverance.

Along the way, each of them faced challenges—some small, others life-altering. Financial hardships, failures, rejections, and doubts were common chapters in their stories. Yet, what set them apart was their refusal to give up. Even when the odds were stacked against them, they held tightly to their vision. They adapted, grew stronger, and kept moving forward. Difficult times became turning points, and setbacks became fuel for greater determination.

What once seemed impossible slowly turned into reality through years of dreaming, planning, and doing. The road to success is rarely straight, but those who dare to dream and never quit eventually find a way. Their stories remind us that greatness is not reserved for the lucky few—it is earned by those who believe in their vision and are willing to work tirelessly to make it happen. The impossible becomes possible for those who never stop trying.

7. STRONG FOUNDATIONS

Edgar was a contractor with a reputation for cutting corners, prioritizing profit over integrity. When he secured a lucrative contract to construct a multistoried office building, the owners trusted him to deliver a safe and durable structure. However, beneath the impressive exterior he presented, Edgar made dangerous compromises. Instead of using the high-grade steel specified in the plans, he opted for low-quality materials to save costs. The finished building looked striking from the outside, with a polished façade that projected an image of strength and elegance, but inside it was a fragile shell waiting to be tested.

That test came sooner than anyone expected. When a mild tremor shook the area, neighboring buildings held firm, their solid foundations withstanding the vibrations with ease. Edgar's structure, however, could not endure the strain. Within moments, the office tower crumbled, collapsing into rubble. What had once been a proud symbol of progress now stood as a grim monument to Edgar's negligence. The collapse exposed not only the weakness of the steel but also the weakness of Edgar's character—reminding everyone that true strength lies in honesty, accountability, and the unseen integrity of what is built beneath the surface.

Just as a building rests securely on its foundation, so too does a human life depend on the strength of its inner base. Our philosophy, values, education, and experiences form the unseen framework that supports who we are. These elements may not always be visible to others, much like the concrete and steel beneath a skyscraper, but they determine whether we stand firm when pressure mounts or collapse when life shakes us. Without strong foundations, even the most impressive outward appearance cannot endure for long.

Every individual, at some point, faces trials that put these foundations to the test. Challenges may come in the form of personal loss, professional setbacks, or moral dilemmas that demand difficult choices. In those moments, superficial charm, wealth, or status provide little protection. Instead, it is the depth of our convictions, the lessons we have absorbed, and the principles we live by that allow us to weather the storms. Just as a tremor reveals the true quality of a structure, hardships reveal the true character of a person.

When our foundations are strong, time itself becomes a proving ground that does not weaken us but rather refines us. The years may bring change, adversity, or uncertainty, yet those anchored in truth, wisdom, and integrity remain steady. They may bend but do not break, and like well-built towers, they rise tall again after each test. Investing in our inner foundation—through continual learning, reflection, and the practice of values—ensures that we are prepared not just to survive, but to endure and inspire others along the way.

8. THE FLAVORS OF LIFE

Food is a universal language enjoyed by people across the globe, transcending borders and cultures. From the elaborate Kerala Sadhya with its variety of vegetarian delicacies served on a banana leaf, to the rich Indian Thali meals offering a balanced combination of flavors, to the comforting strands of Chinese noodles or the creamy richness of European pasta, every cuisine presents a unique palette of tastes that delights the senses. Culinary traditions are not only about nourishment but also about identity, heritage, and celebration, reflecting centuries of history and regional diversity on each plate.

Every meal is carefully crafted to bring balance to the palate, often including dishes that are bland, sour, bitter, spicy, or fiery hot, so that no single taste dominates the dining experience. Water or other beverages are commonly consumed alongside meals to aid digestion and refresh the mouth between flavors. Traditionally, many cultures conclude their meals with a sweet dish—whether it be Indian desserts like payasam, European pastries, or Chinese sweet rice cakes—providing a satisfying sense of closure. In this way, meals become more than sustenance; they are moments of connection, joy, and cultural expression shared across generations.

Life, in many ways, mirrors the experience of enjoying a meal. Just as a meal has a balance of flavors—sweet, sour, spicy, and bitter—life too offers us a mixture of experiences that shape who we are. There are moments of joy and comfort, like the satisfying dishes we savor, but there are also times when we must face challenges, hardships, and disappointments, much like the bitter or overly spicy bites that make us wince. These contrasting experiences add depth and meaning, reminding us that life is not meant to be one-dimensional.

Along the way, we encounter sour relationships or situations that leave us unsettled. There are times when pride must be set aside, just as one might swallow an unpalatable dish for the sake of courtesy or tradition. Learning to let go of ego and adapt to circumstances is part of the larger journey of life. These experiences, although sometimes unpleasant, often help us grow stronger, more patient, and more compassionate, teaching us the importance of humility and resilience.

Yet, just as many meals end with a sweet dish that lingers pleasantly on the tongue, life too holds the promise of sweetness at its conclusion. The struggles, sacrifices, and lessons endured along the way pave the path to fulfillment, whether in the form of personal achievements, meaningful relationships, or inner peace. The sweetness of success or contentment at the end of life is not just a reward but the culmination of everything tasted before—the bitter, the sour, and the bland—all coming together to create a complete and meaningful journey.

9. LIFE IN THE SHADOW OF A VOLCANO

Millions of years ago, the Indian subcontinent was situated deep in the southern hemisphere, far from the lands it would one day shape and influence. It was a time before human history, when the land was dominated by vast expanses of jungle, mountains, and ancient seas. One fateful day, the Indian subcontinent, with a curious spirit, turned to its neighbors and said, "I wish to journey northward, to the fertile lands of the northern hemisphere, where mighty civilizations will rise and flourish."

Antarctica and Australia, two distant and cold lands, chuckled at the subcontinent's audacious dream. "You? Move north? That's an impossible task," they quipped. But the Indian subcontinent was resolute, determined to take its place among the great lands of the north.

When the time came, the subcontinent began its slow but inevitable journey, drifting away from its ancient home. As it moved, it carried with it the treasures of life—flora and fauna that had flourished in its land for millions of years. The earth trembled, and massive cracks began to form along the shifting land. Volcanoes erupted, spewing molten lava into the air, creating new landscapes and changing the face of the earth forever. Over millennia, the volcanic activity shaped the terrain, while new life continued to evolve in the ever-changing environment.

Through this dynamic transformation, life not only survived but thrived. The Indian subcontinent's passage through time left a trail of new ecosystems and untold wonders. And finally, after eons of travel, the subcontinent collided with the great Eurasian landmass, a cataclysmic encounter that brought forth the towering Himalayas. These mighty peaks, formed by the immense pressure of the collision, became the highest mountains on Earth, their snow-capped summits reaching into the sky.

The rise of the Himalayas was more than just a geological event—it also created new habitats for a variety of life forms. And as the land settled into its new position, the Indian subcontinent became a cradle for the growth of civilizations. For thousands of years, diverse peoples, cultures, and empires flourished within its vast borders, building a rich tapestry of human history.

Ever since that incredible journey, the Indian subcontinent has witnessed the rise and fall of different civilizations, the land has been a crossroads for cultures, ideas, and peoples.

The journey of the Indian subcontinent, from its beginnings in the distant southern hemisphere to its current place in the northern hemisphere, is a testament to the power of nature's forces and the resilience of life itself. And as the centuries continue to unfold, the subcontinent remains a land of endless transformation and endless possibility.

Life is the realization of your dreams, the process of turning your aspirations into tangible achievements. These dreams often come in various shapes and sizes, some small and easily attainable, while others may seem vast and distant. It's easy to be discouraged by the magnitude of a dream, especially when it appears impossible to achieve. However, the key to realizing your dreams lies in persistence. Like a river carving its way through rock, the steady, unyielding pursuit of your goals, no matter how lofty they seem, can eventually lead to their fulfillment.

However, the path to your dreams is rarely without obstacles. Just as life flourishes in places of great adversity—whether in the shadows of erupting volcanoes or around the searing heat of oceanic thermal vents—your journey will likely be filled with challenges. These challenges may take the form of setbacks, failures, or external forces working against you. But much like the thriving ecosystems that grow in the harshest environments, your resilience and adaptability can help you not only survive but thrive in the face of difficulties. Life doesn't always follow a smooth path, and it's through overcoming these hurdles that we grow stronger, wiser, and more capable.

In the end, the realization of your dreams is not just about reaching the destination but about how you evolve along the way. Every challenge, every setback, and every moment of doubt is part of the larger journey toward self-discovery and achievement. Embrace the turbulence and uncertainty, for they are the forge in which your strength is tempered. Just as life exists in the most extreme corners of our planet, so too can your dreams take root and flourish even in the most unexpected circumstances. With persistence, patience, and faith in the process, you will find that no dream is too big to reach.

10. ENTHUSIASM: THE KEY TO A SUCCESSFUL LIFE

Bob and his teenage son, Ben, paid a visit to Aunt Molly at her recently purchased home. Nestled beside a sprawling golf course, the house boasted a large, well-kept yard with lush green grass stretching all the way to the property's edge. As they arrived, Aunt Molly warmly welcomed them and encouraged the pair to explore the yard. She cheerfully mentioned that any stray golf balls they found lying around could be theirs to keep. To make the little treasure hunt easier, she handed them a plastic bag to collect whatever they discovered.

Despite the opportunity, Ben wasn't particularly thrilled. A typical teenager, he showed little interest in venturing out or getting involved in what he saw as a boring task. His body language was slouched, and he moved slowly, dragging his feet in quiet protest. Bob, however, was more eager and insisted that Ben join him in exploring the yard. Determined to make the most of the visit, Bob nudged his reluctant son forward and began scanning the grass carefully, hoping to find a few hidden golf balls.

As they wandered through the outer edge of the yard, Bob's attention paid off. He soon spotted a white golf ball nestled in the grass and passed it over to Ben, hoping to encourage him. Energized by the discovery, Bob pressed on and managed to find several more balls scattered along the boundary of the property. Ben, on the other hand, remained half-hearted in his efforts and only managed to locate a single golf ball. He did not even observe a yellow golf ball that he stepped on! In the end, Bob did most of the collecting while Ben trailed behind with minimal enthusiasm, clutching the one ball he'd managed to find on his own.

Enthusiasm is one of the most powerful forces behind a successful life and career. It is the spark that fuels persistence, creativity, and a positive outlook even in the face of adversity. When a person is truly enthusiastic about their goals—whether it's a profession, a project, or a dream—they are more likely to push through obstacles, maintain focus, and stay committed for the long haul. This genuine excitement often inspires others as well, creating a ripple effect that draws support and opportunities.

While intelligence and natural talent are valuable assets, they are not the sole determinants of success. In fact, someone who may not appear as sharp or skilled as their peers can still surpass them through consistent effort and an unwavering sense of enthusiasm. Passionate individuals are more willing to learn, improve, and adapt, often turning weaknesses into strengths. They seek knowledge, embrace challenges, and bring energy to everything they do—traits that are often more valuable than raw intellect alone.

Moreover, enthusiasm can turn failure into a stepping stone rather than a setback. Even when ventures do not go as planned, an enthusiastic person does not view the experience as defeat but rather as a lesson and an opportunity for growth. This mindset fosters resilience and builds character. With each setback, they return with renewed determination and fresh ideas, eventually finding the path to success. In the end, it is not just intelligence or luck, but an enduring enthusiasm that becomes the driving force behind lasting achievement.

11. KEEPING THE DOOR CLOSED FOREVER

Sam lived in a spacious, elegant home nestled on a wide stretch of land. The house was filled with numerous doors, each leading to a different area of the property—some opened to flower-filled gardens, others to winding stone paths or shaded groves. However, one particular door stood apart from the rest. This door, weathered and rarely used, opened out to a marshy, unstable section of the land. The ground beyond it was soft and treacherous, covered in dense reeds and hidden puddles that could easily trap the unwary.

Knowing the danger that lay beyond, Sam made a firm decision: no one should venture through that door. Whether it was visiting friends, curious children, or even household staff, he didn't want anyone stepping foot onto the unpredictable terrain. To ensure everyone's safety, Sam kept the door permanently closed and secured. He didn't just lock it; he sealed it in subtle ways—by rearranging furniture to obscure it, and by quietly discouraging questions about it. To Sam, protecting others from the hidden risks of the marsh was more important than explaining why the door remained unopened. It became a silent boundary in the house, a forgotten threshold guarding against unseen perils.

Some of our deepest vices are incredibly difficult to control. They often become embedded in our habits, our thinking patterns, and even our identities, making them hard to recognize and harder still to overcome. Whether they stem from weakness, pain, pride, or unresolved trauma, these vices can quietly govern our decisions and limit our potential. Breaking free from them requires more than simple willpower; it demands years of intentional effort, a shift in perspective, and often a journey of spiritual or philosophical growth. True transformation begins when we begin to see the world—and ourselves—through a different lens, one shaped by humility, discipline, and self-awareness.

When these vices are finally conquered, the relief and freedom that follow can feel like emerging from a dark, enclosed space into sunlight. Yet with that freedom comes responsibility. Just as one might lock a dangerous gate to protect others from falling into harm, so too must we lock away the past versions of ourselves that were controlled by those vices. There's wisdom in turning away from old temptations, from places and patterns that once ensnared us. Reopening those doors, even in thought, can stir memories and emotions that threaten to undo the progress we've made. The path to healing is fragile, and revisiting the darkness can sometimes be more dangerous than staying in it.

Therefore, once you have broken free, resist the urge to look back. The past should be acknowledged, but not romanticized or revisited. Keep it sealed like a gate that once led to a swamp—dangerous, deceptive, and unnecessary to your current journey. Instead, focus on cultivating the person you've become, rooted in strength, clarity, and peace. Let your growth speak louder than your past struggles, and remember that the true measure of change is not just in escaping old patterns, but in choosing every day not to return to them.

12. LIVING ON OTHERS BLOOD, SWEAT AND TEARS

Brett lived a life of luxury, surrounded by wealth, fame, and admiration from the outside world. Yet behind closed doors, he treated those who worked for him with cruelty and disregard. He underpaid his employees, offering salaries far below industry standards despite his ability to afford more. Worse still, he frequently lashed out at them with verbal abuse whenever their performance failed to meet his rigid expectations. His harsh and exploitative behavior created an environment of fear and resentment, leaving his employees feeling devalued and powerless.

Over time, the bitterness he sowed began to catch up with him. The people he mistreated carried lasting anger, and many cursed him for his misdeeds. As the years passed, Brett's fortune dwindled, his fame faded, and his health declined. Isolated and weakened, he died penniless and forgotten by the very society that once celebrated him. In the end, the luxury he once flaunted could not shield him from the consequences of his actions, serving as a stark reminder that how we treat others often determines the legacy we leave behind.

Wealth and fame, while admirable in the eyes of many, come with a profound responsibility.

When a person achieves success, it is easy to fall into the trap of pride, forgetting the countless people who contributed along the way. True greatness is not measured solely by money or recognition, but by how one treats others, especially those who work behind the scenes. Humility is the anchor that keeps success grounded. It reminds us that no achievement is entirely self-made and that every empire rests on the shoulders of countless hands—each with their own story, struggle, and dignity.

Building a business or legacy should never come at the cost of exploiting others. You cannot, and should not, create an empire on the blood, sweat, and tears of your employees. When workers are underpaid, overworked, or disrespected, it reveals a deeply flawed foundation, no matter how grand the outer structure may seem. An empire built on exploitation may stand tall for a time, but it is unstable and unsustainable. Eventually, the weight of injustice collapses it from within. Respect, fairness, and compassion are the true building blocks of a legacy that lasts.

History is filled with examples of powerful individuals who rose high only to fall because they failed to honor those beneath them. Conversely, those who lead with humility and integrity are remembered not only for their accomplishments but for their humanity.

Treating employees with respect, providing fair wages, and creating a supportive work environment is not just good ethics—it's good leadership. In the end, the measure of a truly successful person lies not in how high they rise, but in how well they lift others along the way.

13. NARROW FOCUS

Isidor was the CEO of a mid-sized company employing over 2,000 people. On paper, he was a competent leader—decisive, results-driven, and focused. Yet in practice, his leadership had a glaring blind spot: he had little connection with the majority of his workforce. His attention was reserved exclusively for his direct reports—senior managers who filtered the information he received. As a result, Isidor had no real sense of what most employees actually did or how they felt about their work.

Many within the company quietly resented this distance. They saw Isidor as distant and aloof—not a "people's CEO," but rather a figurehead who steered the ship from a closed-off captain's cabin.

Then one ordinary morning, something unusual happened—Isidor's car wouldn't start. Left without his usual mode of transportation, he reluctantly ordered a ride share. As he sat in the passenger seat, he gazed out the window, taking in the scenery with uncharacteristic attentiveness. To his surprise, he noticed beautiful homes nestled along tree-lined streets, lively parks filled with morning joggers, and bustling local businesses—places he had driven past for years without ever really seeing.

It struck him then: for so long, he had been so focused on the road ahead—on getting from point A to point B—that he had completely ignored the world around him. The revelation made him uncomfortable. He began to wonder if the same narrow focus had affected how he led his company.

When he arrived at the office that day, something shifted. Sitting alone in his glass-walled corner office, Isidor reflected deeply. He realized he had been treating his company like a highway—focusing only on high-level metrics and milestones, while ignoring the human landscape that kept everything running.

Over the weeks that followed, Isidor made a conscious effort to change. He began walking the floors, introducing himself to employees by name, asking about their roles, challenges, and ideas. He scheduled regular town halls and created anonymous feedback channels. He celebrated small wins publicly and took time to recognize individual contributions. Gradually, a cultural transformation took root.

The change wasn't just felt—it was measured. Employee engagement soared. Retention rates improved. And most notably, the company's performance began to climb, growing by an impressive 10% each quarter. But more than the numbers, it was the renewed sense of connection and shared purpose that defined Isidor's success.

He had finally seen the landscape—and this time, he wasn't just passing through.

14. LESSONS FROM THE LIFE OF A LEAF

The leaf is the fundamental unit of a plant, playing a crucial role in its overall vitality and growth. Through processes like photosynthesis, the leaf captures sunlight and converts it into energy, fueling the plant's development. The condition of the leaves often mirrors the well-being of the plant itself—healthy, vibrant leaves indicate a thriving organism, while damaged or wilting leaves are signs of distress. In this way, a single leaf, though small, serves as a powerful symbol of life and sustenance in the natural world.

When a leaf reaches full maturity, it becomes a striking example of natural beauty. Lush in color and rich in texture, it contributes to the plant's visual splendor and ecological function. As the seasons change, particularly in autumn, the leaf undergoes a transformation. Its green pigments give way to brilliant hues of red, orange, and yellow. This vibrant transition marks the beginning of its final phase. Eventually, the leaf dries at the edges, detaches from the branch, and gently falls to the ground.

Yet the story of the leaf does not end with its fall. On the forest floor, fallen leaves are not discarded waste but are integral to the life cycle of the ecosystem. Microorganisms begin to break down the leaf matter, transforming it into rich organic material. This decomposition process rejuvenates the soil, providing nutrients that support new growth in the coming seasons. Thus, the leaf's life, though finite, contributes directly to the renewal and continuation of plant life.

In many ways, the life cycle of a leaf mirrors the human experience. A man, like a leaf, begins life full of potential and beauty, reaching his prime in youth and gradually aging over time. Though his physical form may wither, his impact can live on. Unlike the leaf, whose contributions nourish the soil physically, a human being leaves behind something deeper and less tangible—an enduring legacy of values, love, and wisdom. While the body may perish, the moral compass a person instills in others, the lessons shared, and the kindness shown can take root in the hearts and minds of future generations. These lasting impressions ripple through time, influencing children, grandchildren, and even communities in ways both seen and unseen. In this way, though a man's life may end, the essence of his character lives on, continuing to shape the world just as surely as the decomposed leaf nourishes the roots of a new season's growth.

15. STREET SMART

When Miya received an urgent invitation to speak at a professional conference in a distant city, she had little time to prepare. With no one else available to look after her children on such short notice, she quickly called her dependable Aunt Nancy for help. Without hesitation, Aunt Nancy packed a bag and arrived later that day, ready to take charge.

No sooner had she stepped through the door than the children approached her with a pressing concern of their own. They needed to bake a loaf of raisin bread for a school food drive scheduled for the next morning. Miya had promised to help them, but now the responsibility had passed to Aunt Nancy.

Without wasting a moment, Aunt Nancy rolled up her sleeves and began gathering ingredients from the kitchen. She measured the flour, cracked the eggs, and started preparing the dough with practiced hands. But just as she reached for the container of raisins, she realized something alarming—it was nearly empty. There were only a few shriveled raisins left at the bottom of the jar.

Thinking quickly, Aunt Nancy turned to the children and asked, "Do we have any raisin cereal? Like raisin corn flakes?"

The children exchanged glances and then dashed to the pantry. Moments later, they triumphantly returned with not one but two unopened boxes of raisin corn flakes.

"Perfect!" Aunt Nancy exclaimed.

She grabbed a large, clean plate and poured out both boxes of cereal. Carefully and patiently, she began separating the raisins from the flakes, setting each plump piece aside in a small bowl. It took a little time, but eventually, she had just enough raisins for the recipe. Once done, she neatly repacked the corn flakes and returned them to the pantry for later use.

With the necessary ingredient in hand, Aunt Nancy folded the rescued raisins into the dough, shaped the loaf, and placed it into the oven. The warm scent of cinnamon and baked bread soon filled the kitchen, drawing the children close with eager anticipation.

When the raisin bread finally emerged from the oven, golden brown and fragrant, everyone agreed—it looked and smelled wonderful. The next day, the children proudly carried their homemade raisin bread to school, knowing they had made it together with a little ingenuity, a lot of teamwork, and the love of their Aunt Nancy.

Sometimes in life, being book smart—knowing facts, theories, and academic concepts—isn't enough to get you through real-world challenges. While classroom knowledge is valuable, life often throws unpredictable situations your way where there's no textbook to guide you. This is where street smarts come in. Being street smart means having the awareness and instinct to handle unexpected problems with confidence and clarity within split-second. It's about quickly analyzing your environment, understanding people's intentions, and making smart choices without hesitation. Whether you're figuring out how to get home when your phone dies or calming a tense conversation, street smarts equip you to navigate life's messier, unscripted moments.

What sets street-smart individuals apart is their ability to remain composed under pressure and act decisively. They trust their instincts but also rely on past experiences and keen observation. In fast-paced situations—like avoiding a scam, de-escalating a conflict, or making a split-second decision in traffic—there's no time to second-guess. The ability to adapt, improvise, and respond with a level head can not only solve problems efficiently but also keep you safe. In many ways, street smarts are a different kind of intelligence—one rooted in common sense, emotional awareness, and quick thinking.

16. PERSPECTIVE

An artist once created an abstract painting intended to represent the powerful act of compassion—someone extending help to a person in desperate need during a dire situation. Rather than using literal imagery, the artist chose abstraction to evoke emotion and thought, hoping to capture the essence of human empathy in times of crisis. The piece was given the title Perspective, emphasizing that the meaning behind the artwork was not fixed, but fluid—shaped by the eyes and minds of those who beheld it. The artist deliberately avoided a detailed explanation, leaving room for personal interpretation and reflection.

As viewers stood before the painting, each brought their own experiences, beliefs, and emotions, which colored their interpretation. Some perceived chaos and struggle and concluded the image portrayed the horrors of war, while others saw darkness and distortion, suggesting it reflected the workings of a disturbed or malevolent mind. These varied reactions illustrated the artist's core message—that every individual sees the world through a unique lens. Through this ambiguity, the artwork not only invited diverse readings but also highlighted the complexity and subjectivity of human perception.

Every person you encounter in life will form an opinion about you, whether consciously or unconsciously. These judgments are often shaped quickly and with limited information. While some individuals take the time to observe your actions, behavior, and the way you treat others before forming an impression, many rely heavily on superficial cues—your appearance, facial expressions, clothing, or the way you carry yourself. These surface-level assessments may not reflect your true character or intentions, yet they play a powerful role in shaping how others perceive you.

Unfortunately, the human tendency to judge based on outward appearances often leads to misunderstandings and misjudgments. A kind heart, a generous spirit, or a deeply thoughtful mind can easily be overlooked if it doesn't fit into someone's preconceived notions or expectations. The truth is, no one can fully understand the complexities of another person. People may assume they know who you are based on fragments of what they see, but those assumptions often fall short of the reality. We live in a world where image can overshadow substance, and this makes it all the more important to remain true to yourself, regardless of how others see you.

Ultimately, only you truly know who you are at your core. Even those closest to you—your parents, your spouse, your children—might not fully grasp the depths of your thoughts, struggles, dreams, or fears. Your inner world is shaped by countless experiences, reflections, and emotions that cannot be easily communicated or understood by others. That's why it's essential to cultivate a strong sense of self, independent of others' opinions. Embrace your individuality and find peace in the knowledge that your worth is not determined by how others perceive you, but by who you are when no one else is watching.

17. LEADING THROUGH THE STORM

Toby and his friends were on their way home after a grueling soccer (football) match. The mood inside the car was anything but cheerful. Their team had suffered a disappointing defeat, dashing any hopes of qualifying for the finals. Frustration hung thick in the air, and before long, tempers flared. What began as heated words quickly escalated into shouting, and then some of the friends started pushing and shoving each other in the back seats.

Despite the chaos around him, Toby remained focused behind the wheel. He gripped the steering wheel tightly, his eyes fixed on the road. He knew that even a moment of distraction could have catastrophic consequences. The car sped along the highway, and one wrong move could result in a serious accident, causing injury—or worse, death. While his friends argued and wrestled in their frustration, Toby stayed calm and vigilant, determined to get everyone home safely.

As an adult, you may one day find yourself in a position of leadership—perhaps as the head of a family or at the helm of an organization. With such responsibility comes both honor and challenge. While some members may admire your guidance and decisions, others may not show the same level of respect. In times of difficulty, especially during moments of failure or uncertainty, tensions can rise. People may direct their frustrations toward you simply because you're the one in charge, and leadership often becomes a lightning rod during turbulent times.

When you are in such a leadership role, it's crucial not to let emotions cloud your judgment. You must remain composed, even when it feels like the world around you is unraveling. Mental distraction or panic can worsen the situation, potentially turning a temporary hardship into a lasting crisis. Just as a driver must stay focused on the road regardless of the noise and chaos inside the car, a leader must keep their eyes on the bigger picture— navigating the group through uncertainty with calm, clarity, and purpose.

Most importantly, never lose sight of hope. Every storm, no matter how fierce, eventually passes. The same is true for the difficult phases a family or organization might face. As the leader, your ability to persevere with strength and optimism can inspire others to do the same. In the darkest moments, your steadiness may be the guiding light that brings everyone through to brighter days. Leadership is not just about making decisions—it's about holding the line gracefully when others are ready to give up.

18. WHEN EFFORT OUTSHINES OPPORTUNITY

Paul and Peter had been close friends and business partners for several years. They often collaborated on small ventures, but one day they decided to take a bold leap into the world of filmmaking. Paul, who had accumulated significant wealth through his past ventures, chose to go all out. With a grand vision in mind, he hired the most qualified technicians, rented high-end equipment, and brought in top-tier actors and celebrities. He believed that with enough investment, success was guaranteed. The production of his film was lavish, with elaborate sets, expensive costumes, and a marketing campaign that captured the public's attention long before the movie was even released.

On the other hand, Peter approached the project quite differently. Though he lacked financial resources, he was passionate about the art of storytelling. A gifted writer and creative thinker, Peter penned a deeply emotional and thought-provoking script that drew from real-life experiences. Without the luxury of a big budget, he turned to aspiring actors and amateur crew members who shared his vision and were eager to prove themselves. What they lacked in experience, they made up for in enthusiasm and authenticity. The production was humble, shot in real locations with minimal props and simple costumes, but the emotional depth of the story gave it a soul.

When both movies hit the theaters, the results were surprising. Despite the high expectations and star-studded cast, Paul's mega movie fell flat with audiences. Critics panned it for lacking substance, saying it was all spectacle with no heart. Meanwhile, Peter's modest film struck a chord with viewers. Its sincerity, relatable characters, and meaningful storyline resonated deeply, leading to rave reviews and packed theaters. Word of mouth spread quickly, and Peter's film became a super hit, dominating the box office for months. In the end, it was a powerful reminder that while money can buy resources, it is genuine creativity and emotional connection that win the hearts of the audience.

In many affluent families, parents invest heavily in their children's development, sparing no expense in the hopes of crafting a bright and successful future. These children are often enrolled in prestigious private schools with top-tier facilities and well-trained teachers. Their schedules are packed with extracurricular activities like soccer, swimming, guitar lessons, horse riding, karate, and robotics classes— each one seen as a stepping stone to excellence. While these opportunities are certainly valuable, some of these children, despite all the resources and guidance, grow up without a strong sense of direction or purpose. Surrounded by constant structure and parental pressure, they may lack the internal drive to push beyond what is given to them, and as adults, they sometimes fade into mediocrity—becoming what society might call a "Mr. Nobody."

In contrast, children from less privileged families often grow up in environments where opportunities are limited and resources are scarce. Yet, within these constraints, a powerful sense of determination can blossom. Without access to elite programs or expensive lessons, these children take it upon themselves to seek knowledge and growth. They frequent public libraries, study independently, and find creative ways to explore their interests. Their motivation is not driven by parental expectation, but by their own desire to rise above their circumstances. They learn to solve problems, manage time, and persevere through hardship—all of which become valuable traits as they move through life.

Over time, the resilience and self-motivation developed in these humble beginnings often lead to remarkable achievements. These individuals may not have started with privilege, but their grit and initiative propel them forward. They become innovators, leaders, and change makers—the very people others look up to. In the end, it is not the price tag of a child's education or the number of activities on their résumé that determines their future, but rather the character, drive, and curiosity they carry within them. And thus, many of these underdog children, shaped by struggle and fueled by ambition, grow into a "Mr. Somebody."

19. THE UNCHANGING WINDS OF HUMAN NATURE

Sailing ships were remarkable feats of early maritime engineering, powered solely by the wind. Their tall masts held expansive sails that could be adjusted to catch breezes from various angles, allowing sailors to maneuver across vast oceans. Through careful navigation and strategic use of wind patterns, these vessels were able to travel great distances— even against moderate resistance. Long before the arrival of steamships, sailing ships ruled the seas, playing a vital role in global commerce, exploration, and military conquest. Their effectiveness depended heavily on wind strength and direction, making each voyage a blend of science, skill, and chance. These wind-driven vessels not only shaped trade routes but also played a central role in shaping the course of human history. Entire continents were discovered, mapped, colonized, and connected through the journeys of sailing ships. The history and geography of the Earth, as we know it today, were deeply influenced by their paths. They opened up new worlds, facilitated cultural exchanges, and laid the groundwork for the modern global economy.

However, sailing ships had a major limitation— they were at the mercy of the elements. If the wind died down or became too erratic, the ships would slow to a crawl or drift aimlessly. In such situations, they could only rely on the ocean currents to move them forward, which offered little control and made it difficult to stay on course. This dependence on natural forces made sailing a challenging endeavor, often causing delays and dangers in reaching the intended destination. The invention of steamships revolutionized sea travel, offering consistent power regardless of weather and effectively ending the dominance of traditional sail-driven vessels.

Human nature has remained remarkably consistent since the dawn of civilization. While we have made extraordinary strides in science, medicine, transportation, and communication, the core traits that define us have hardly changed. Emotions such as love, hatred, jealousy, fear, compassion, and kindness have always been central to the human experience. From ancient tribal societies to modern urban centers, people continue to experience the same emotional struggles, ethical dilemmas, and moral triumphs. These traits are timeless, passed down through generations, shaping human behavior regardless of the era or the tools we use.

As technology has evolved—from stone tools to smartphones, from fire to nuclear energy—the emotional and psychological makeup of humans has remained largely intact. The stage may be different, with artificial intelligence, space travel, and digital communication setting the backdrop, but the drama of humanity remains the same. Acts of treachery and betrayal still occur, just as they did in ancient myths and legends. Altruism, empathy, and heroic self-sacrifice continue to inspire us, just as they did in tales of ancient heroes. The tools we use have changed drastically, but the hands that wield them are driven by the same inner forces that moved our ancestors.

In essence, these enduring human traits are like the wind that propels the vessel of civilization forward. They fuel our passions, drive our decisions, and shape the course of history. Whether it is a tale of love in a medieval village or a conflict driven by envy in a boardroom skyscraper, the underlying emotions remain the same. Humanity's technological background may have transformed over millennia, but our emotional foreground—our character—remains a powerful, unchanging force that continues to define the human story.

20. INTEGRITY IN A CROOKED WORLD

Planter Thompson faced a significant challenge when one of his most valued clients placed a special request: 25-meter-long teak logs that had to be perfectly straight—without the slightest bend or curve. This wasn't an ordinary order; such specifications required an exceptionally rare tree, one that had grown tall and true over decades without deviation. The client's demand coupled with premium pricing placed immense pressure on Thompson, as fulfilling it would not only maintain the client's trust but also enhance his reputation as a premium supplier of high-grade teak wood.

Determined to meet the request, Thompson began a meticulous search through his vast plantation, which spanned hundreds of mature teak trees. Despite the abundance of trees, he quickly realized how rare perfectly straight specimens were. After several days of surveying the land, measuring trunks, and checking for flaws, he managed to identify only twenty-five trees that met the necessary standards of straightness. Though he was relieved to have found a few options, the narrow margin meant he had to carefully select the best among them—one that not only measured up in size but also in quality, grain uniformity, and structural integrity.

Crookedness, in its many forms, is often seen as an ingrained aspect of human nature. From subtle deceptions to outright dishonesty, the tendency to bend truth or behave unethically seems to have existed throughout history. While society teaches ideals of honesty and integrity, the reality is that human behavior often deviates from these principles, especially when personal gain, power, or survival is at stake. This inherent flaw does not always manifest in dramatic or criminal ways—it can appear in everyday actions, such as cutting corners, telling half-truths, or manipulating situations to one's advantage.

In the modern age, finding a person entirely free of crookedness is increasingly rare. With the rise of competition, social pressures, and the digital world's anonymity, people are frequently tempted to present a version of themselves that is not entirely genuine. Social media encourages curated lives; business environments often reward results over ethics; and political discourse is frequently marked by spin rather than substance. Even in personal relationships, manipulation and misrepresentation can sometimes replace honesty and transparency. These behaviors, while often rationalized or overlooked, reflect the subtle and pervasive nature of crookedness in contemporary society.

Yet, despite this prevailing condition, there remains a deep respect and longing for individuals who live with integrity. People who act with consistent honesty, fairness, and moral clarity often stand out—not because they are the norm, but precisely because they are rare. Their character becomes a benchmark and a source of inspiration, reminding others that while crookedness may be common, it is not inevitable. In a world that often rewards expediency over ethics, the choice to remain straight and principled is both courageous and commendable.

21. ADDING COLOR IN YOUR LIFE

In the early stages of life, many people often find themselves caught in a routine that feels monotonous and uninspiring. Days may blend together with school, work, or responsibilities that offer little excitement or emotional fulfillment. This sense of boredom or stagnation is a common human experience, especially when one is still trying to discover their identity, passions, or purpose. Life can feel predictable and gray when each day seems like a mere repetition of the last, and the future appears uncertain or too far away to grasp.

Yet, life does not have to remain this way. There are people who enter our lives—teachers, mentors, and advisors—who can light a spark and help us see the world through a new, more vibrant lens. These individuals bring wisdom, encouragement, and sometimes even a sense of direction. A good teacher might awaken a love for learning, a mentor might offer guidance through life's complexities, and an advisor may help us identify and pursue meaningful goals. These relationships often inject color and hope into our lives, turning what once felt dull into something rich with purpose and potential.

However, not everyone who claims to bring joy or meaning into your life does so with genuine intentions. There are those who present themselves as entertaining, charismatic figures, often offering quick-fix solutions to happiness or success. They may promise instant wealth, popularity, or fulfillment, drawing you in with charm and exaggerated promises. These individuals often appeal to the desire for a more colorful and exciting life, but what they offer is artificial and fleeting—a kind of pseudocolor that fades once the novelty wears off or when consequences surface.

It's important to discern between those who genuinely enrich your life and those who merely provide a temporary illusion. Real mentors and guides build you up with honesty, substance, and steady encouragement, while the pseudo-guides dazzle you momentarily but leave you confused, disappointed, or even worse off. In the journey of life, finding true color comes not from shortcuts or superficial pleasures, but from meaningful relationships, personal growth, and the steady pursuit of what is good and true.

22. BEYOND YOUR CONTROL

Edwin was a technologist at a mid-sized firm, where he led a small but dedicated team. Despite his relatively modest position, he regularly contributed original and forward-thinking ideas that had the potential to transform key processes within the company. However, his creativity was not welcomed by the chief technologist, who viewed Edwin's initiatives with suspicion and repeatedly dismissed them without consideration. The lack of support and appreciation left Edwin disillusioned, particularly when one of his most promising proposals—an innovation that could have significantly enhanced operational efficiency—was outright rejected.

Frustrated but determined, Edwin decided to leave the company and explore new opportunities. He began applying to several organizations and was eventually invited for an interview at a large, global firm. During the interview, Edwin presented his vision and outlined the same innovative ideas that had been previously overlooked. Impressed by his clarity and potential, the company hired him on a temporary basis, granting him two years to bring his project to life. Wasting no time, Edwin assembled a new team, including a few trusted former colleagues, and completed the ambitious project in just six months. The resulting technology not only succeeded but generated immense profits for the company, establishing Edwin as a key asset.

Recognizing his impact, the company quickly promoted Edwin to Chief Technology Officer. As the company operated across multiple continents, he was even provided with a private aircraft to support his frequent international engagements. Edwin's influence extended beyond internal innovation—he became a strategic advisor to client companies, helping them enhance their own products and services. His ability to deliver tangible results while fostering long-term vision earned him the admiration of the board. In due course, Edwin was elevated to the role of Chief Executive Officer, a position from which he continued to drive transformative growth across the organization and its partners.

Sometimes in life, we encounter events that spiral beyond our ability to manage or influence. No matter how carefully we plan or how diligently we work, there are moments when unforeseen circumstances disrupt our path. These could come in the form of personal loss, professional setbacks, or sudden changes in health, relationships, or finances. The feeling of helplessness in such moments can be overwhelming, making us question our efforts and intentions. But it's important to understand that not everything in life is within our grasp, and sometimes surrendering control is not weakness—it is wisdom.

When situations slip out of our hands, the best course of action may be to stop resisting and allow time to take the reins. Time has an incredible way of healing wounds, offering clarity, and rearranging life in ways we never imagined. Instead of reacting in haste or frustration, waiting with patience and faith can provide new perspectives and open doors that once seemed shut. By trusting time, we also give ourselves room to breathe, reflect, and recover. Letting go doesn't mean giving up—it means creating space for new possibilities to unfold.

Ultimately, allowing time to guide us through uncontrollable situations teaches resilience and humility. It reminds us that life is not always about forcing outcomes, but about adapting and growing through uncertainty. Many of the most beautiful chapters in life are born out of difficult periods where time was our only ally. So when things go beyond your control, take a step back, lean on patience, and let time gently show the way forward. In the end, what seems like a detour might lead you exactly where you need to be.

23. BUILD YOUR CHAIR

In today's fiercely competitive world, landing a stable, full-time job is becoming increasingly difficult—especially for those just starting out. For many, the first step into the professional world begins with an internship. These internships can be either paid or unpaid, but regardless of compensation, they offer a critical opportunity to demonstrate your skills, work ethic, and potential. However, merely having an internship isn't enough. What truly matters is how you use that opportunity to stand out.

Some interns treat their internships passively— they arrive on time, sit in the chair provided, and complete only the tasks they are directly assigned. These individuals do the bare minimum, waiting for instructions, avoiding extra responsibilities, and failing to take initiative. While they may believe that simply fulfilling their basic duties is enough to earn a job offer, companies often see otherwise. At the end of the internship, when these individuals ask about full-time opportunities, they are often told that there are no openings available. In truth, it's not the lack of positions, but the lack of initiative that holds them back.

On the other hand, standout interns come with a different mindset. They don't just sit in the chair—they build their own. They observe the company's needs, take initiative, ask thoughtful questions, and go beyond what is expected of them. These interns understand that the internship is not just a temporary task but a platform to prove their worth. They suggest improvements, offer innovative ideas, and make themselves indispensable. In doing so, they begin to shape a role for themselves—one that didn't exist before but now can't be ignored.

Companies recognize and reward such individuals. When someone consistently adds value, demonstrates commitment, and contributes positively to the work environment, decision-makers take notice. These are the interns who often receive job offers before their internships even end. The company sees the potential, the dedication, and the forward-thinking attitude—and they don't want to let it go. They create opportunities for those who prove they are worth investing in.

So, don't just settle into the seat you're given. Build your own chair—construct it with effort, creativity, resilience, and initiative. The more you invest in the process, the more likely you are to turn a short-term role into a long-term opportunity. In a world full of uncertainty, the one thing you can control is how much value you bring. And when you build your chair, you're not just applying for a job—you're creating a place for yourself in the professional world.

24. INTEGRITY IN THE WORKPLACE

Ted applied for a job at a contracting company and was soon hired to assist with various field projects. As part of his responsibilities, the senior contractor entrusted him with a company-owned truck to transport tools and equipment to job sites. This gesture demonstrated the company's trust in Ted's reliability and professionalism. Ted was known for maintaining his personal vehicle meticulously, so it was expected he would treat the company truck with the same level of care and responsibility.

However, once in possession of the truck, Ted showed a surprising disregard for its condition. He drove recklessly, frequently speeding over potholes and uneven roads, failed to take the vehicle in for scheduled maintenance, and generally handled it with carelessness. Over time, the damage accumulated, and the truck eventually broke down, requiring costly repairs. When the company reviewed the cause, they discovered Ted's pattern of negligent behavior. His lack of respect for company property and poor judgment led management to lose confidence in him, and ultimately, he was terminated. The situation served as a reminder that trust in the workplace must be matched with accountability and respect for shared resources.

Some individuals take great care of their personal belongings, treating their cars, electronics, and homes with attention and responsibility. However, when it comes to company property, they often behave differently—careless with equipment, wasteful with supplies, and indifferent to maintenance. This mindset, where people value only what they personally own, creates a hidden but serious problem in workplaces. Misusing or neglecting company assets doesn't just harm the business; it leads to increased operational costs, which ultimately get passed down to consumers in the form of higher prices. It also fosters a culture of wastefulness and irresponsibility, weakening the overall efficiency and integrity of the organization.

Even small, seemingly harmless actions—like taking extra napkins in a cafeteria or printing unnecessary pages—can have broader consequences. Using more than necessary contributes to excess waste, higher energy consumption, and greater environmental strain. Companies often absorb these costs initially, but over time, they adjust by raising product prices or cutting services. This not only affects consumers but also harms the planet. Respecting company resources is acting with integrity, reducing waste, and contributing to a more sustainable and responsible workplace culture.

25. DETERMINATION, DISCIPLINE, ALTRUISM

Ken and his father began their journey as humble neighborhood bakers. From their spacious home kitchen, they prepared small batches of cakes, cookies, and chips that were sold to local corner and convenience stores. Baking was not just their livelihood but also an act of service; a portion of their fresh goods was always set aside for the local soup kitchen and old-age home. On weekends, Ken would bring more than food—he brought music. Sitting at the piano, he played cheerful tunes for the residents of the old-age home, creating moments of warmth and companionship that endeared him and his family to the community.

Over time, their reputation for producing high-quality baked goods spread beyond their immediate neighborhood. The superior taste and consistency of their products caught the eye of large retailers, who soon placed daily orders that far exceeded the capacity of their home kitchen. To meet the demand, Ken partnered with a commercial bakery to scale production while maintaining their signature quality. Success quickly multiplied as flight kitchens began purchasing their cakes and cookies to serve on commercial flights, expanding the reach of their baked goods far beyond the local community.

Ken, driven by both passion and curiosity, immersed himself in the broader world of baking. He regularly attended trade shows, built relationships with farmers and mill owners, and honed his expertise through specialized baking classes. Recognizing the importance of innovation, he established a dedicated research and development team by hiring some of the most skilled bakers in the industry. When the opportunity arose to purchase a struggling large food company, Ken seized it, transforming it into a thriving enterprise. Through persistence, vision, and a commitment to quality, Ken's once small family endeavor grew into the largest baking goods company in the country, admired for its roots in community and excellence.

Determination, discipline, and altruism together form one of the most powerful character traits a person can develop. Determination fuels the drive to keep moving forward even in the face of obstacles, while discipline ensures consistency, structure, and the ability to stay focused on long-term goals. Altruism, on the other hand, adds a deeper dimension—it reminds us that our efforts are not just for personal gain but also to uplift others. When these three qualities are woven together, they create a foundation of strength and purpose that can withstand challenges and inspire resilience.

This unique combination does more than bring individual achievement—it creates lasting impact. Determination ensures that goals are pursued with unwavering energy, discipline provides the steady habits that turn vision into reality, and altruism keeps success grounded in service and compassion. A person who embodies these traits becomes not only a high achiever but also a source of inspiration and support to others. Their victories are not selfish milestones but shared triumphs that enrich their community and environment.

Throughout history, individuals who rose to greatness often displayed these three attributes in balance. From leaders who built nations to entrepreneurs who transformed industries, their determination kept them moving forward, their discipline kept them consistent, and their altruism kept them connected to humanity. In modern times, anyone who cultivates this triad of virtues can rise above mediocrity and leave behind a legacy of success that is both meaningful and enduring. Ultimately, determination, discipline, and altruism together form a roadmap not only to personal greatness but also to collective progress.

26. CHASING THE WRONG BUTTERFLY

Dave's mother handed him a small package wrapped in cloth—it contained his uncle's medicine and a bit of food. His uncle, who had fallen ill, lived at the far edge of the village, past the woods and over the meadow. Without hesitation, Dave took the bundle and set off, his steps light with purpose. The sun was warm, the sky clear, and the gentle rustle of the trees made the journey feel almost like an adventure. But as he reached the open meadow where the path curved like a ribbon through tall grass, something caught his eye— a large, brilliant butterfly fluttering in the sunlight. Its wings shimmered with colors Dave had never seen before. Entranced, he followed it, the package tucked under one arm, all thoughts of his errand momentarily forgotten.

What Dave didn't know was that this butterfly was nearing the end of its brief life. It danced through the air, drifting toward a large, wild bush at the edge of the field. Dave chased it eagerly, his heart pounding not with urgency, but wonder. When the butterfly finally vanished into the dense green leaves, Dave approached quietly, expecting it to flutter back out again. But minutes passed. Then more. He searched the bush carefully, pushing aside branches and leaves, peering into every shadow. At last, he found it—its wings now still, the vivid color faded slightly in the golden light. Dave knelt beside it, both in awe and sorrow, realizing he had just witnessed the final moments of something beautiful. Clutching the now slightly crumpled package, he stood slowly, reminded of why he had come and the importance of returning to his journey.

Every person is born with a unique mission—a purpose that gives meaning to their life and direction to their journey. This mission may not always be clear at first; it often takes time, reflection, and experiences to uncover. It's not something handed to us, but something we must seek out with intention. Finding it requires listening to our inner voice, paying attention to what moves our heart, and recognizing the impact we are meant to make in the lives of others.

However, many people get caught chasing the wrong things—wealth without meaning, popularity without purpose, or success defined by others. These pursuits may appear fulfilling for a time, but they often lead us away from our true path. When we invest ourselves in what lacks depth or value, we waste not only our time but also our potential. The energy spent on empty goals could have been used to grow, to serve, or to create something meaningful.

In the end, running after the wrong things doesn't just delay our mission—it can lead us somewhere that benefit no one, not even ourselves. We may find ourselves in places that feel hollow, having achieved what the world values, yet feeling incomplete. Our mission is not about being busy, impressive, or admired. It's about being true to who we are and doing what we are meant to do. Only when we stop chasing shadows and start seeking substance can we step into the life we were truly meant to live.

27. TIME BUDGET

Grandpa Joe came to stay with his daughter Sara for a couple of weeks, and during his visit, he noticed her frustration with her son Arnold. Sara often complained that Arnold was lazy and uninterested in his studies. Instead of focusing on schoolwork, he spent most of his time scrolling through social media or playing with friends, leaving little energy for anything productive. Grandpa Joe, with his gentle wisdom, decided to observe Arnold closely for a few days before stepping in with guidance.

After watching Arnold's routine, Grandpa Joe asked him to record his daily activities in detail—every minute of his schedule. At first, Arnold resisted, feeling it was unnecessary, but eventually he gave in and wrote everything down in a notebook. Together, Grandpa Joe and Arnold went through the list, carefully examining how he spent his time. The results were eye-opening: Arnold spent over six hours on social media, four hours on games and sports, but had almost no time dedicated to reading, writing, or studying. Grandpa Joe explained how time, once wasted, could never be recovered and emphasized the importance of budgeting it wisely.

To help Arnold build better habits, Grandpa Joe created a structured timetable. It included thirty minutes of creative writing, thirty minutes of reading the news, an hour for book reading, and four hours of focused study each day. Sara joined in the effort by teaching Arnold computer programming for thirty minutes daily. With this disciplined approach, Arnold gradually transformed. His creativity blossomed through writing, and his technical skills grew with programming. In time, he became an accomplished author and programmer, publishing dozens of books and developing software that was widely used in business—an inspiring testament to how guidance, discipline, and proper time management can change a life.

Just as financial budgeting helps people manage their money wisely, time budgeting plays an equally vital role in managing life effectively. Money that is spent recklessly often leads to debt and financial stress, while time that is wasted on unproductive activities leads to missed opportunities and unfulfilled potential. Every person is given the same twenty-four hours each day, yet the difference between success and stagnation often lies in how those hours are allocated. Time budgeting encourages people to prioritize what truly matters—whether it is studying, working, exercising, or nurturing relationships—so that no moment is squandered without purpose.

When practiced consistently, time budgeting becomes a powerful tool for balance and growth. By assigning specific periods for learning, leisure, rest, and creativity, individuals avoid the trap of procrastination and make steady progress toward their goals. Just as a financial budget ensures savings and future security, a time budget creates discipline and a sense of accomplishment, ensuring that one's days are meaningful rather than wasted. Ultimately, those who value their time as much as their money often achieve greater success, not only because of their efficiency but also because they learn to live life with intention and clarity.

28. SPEED: THE BACKBONE OF EFFECTIVE PROJECT MANAGEMENT

Stanislav and his mother Jane took on the rewarding task of growing their own vegetables in the backyard. With careful planning and a shared enthusiasm for gardening, they began their project in early spring. By early April, they had already sown various vegetable seeds in pots, providing them a protected start indoors. As the weather warmed, they transplanted the young seedlings into raised beds at the end of April, ensuring they had enough space and good soil to thrive.

Once the plants were settled in their new beds, Jane and Stanislav maintained a consistent care routine. They watered the vegetables regularly to keep the soil moist and supplemented the plants with fertilizers to boost their growth. As is common in gardening, weeds occasionally sprouted up between the vegetable plants, competing for nutrients. The pair diligently removed these invaders to keep the beds healthy and productive. Their efforts paid off—within about 100 days of transplanting, they were able to begin harvesting a satisfying yield of fresh vegetables.

Most of the crops they chose were fast-growing annual vegetables, which are known for their short life cycles. These plants grow quickly, flower, set fruit, and become ready for harvest within a few months. However, this rapid growth comes with a critical need for timely care. Any delays in sowing, transplanting, watering, or fertilizing can significantly impact both the quantity and quality of the produce. For annuals, every phase is time-sensitive, and Stanislav and Jane's success was a direct result of their careful attention to timing and detail throughout the growing season.

Speed is a critical factor in the successful execution of any project. Projects are inherently time-sensitive, often governed by strict deadlines and milestones that must be met to stay on track. Any delay—whether due to poor planning, resource constraints, or unforeseen obstacles—can result in significant consequences. These may include increased costs due to extended labor, missed market opportunities, or even the complete failure of the project. In fast-paced industries, timing can be the difference between staying ahead of the competition and falling behind.

In today's global economy, the availability of resources, including labor, is no longer limited by geography. Businesses can hire talent, source materials, and implement services from virtually any part of the world. This global accessibility increases competition and sets a higher standard for efficiency. If a team or company fails to deliver on time, clients and investors have the option to shift their business elsewhere, often in a matter of days. This puts additional pressure on project managers and teams to deliver results promptly and without excuses.

Moreover, in fields that rely on rapidly evolving technology, such as software development, biotech, or renewable energy, delays can render a project obsolete. Technologies become redundant quickly, and a late release can mean launching a product that is no longer competitive or compatible with current systems. Speed, therefore, is not just about saving time or money—it's about maintaining relevance, seizing opportunities, and ensuring long-term success in a highly dynamic environment.

29. THE HUMAN JOURNEY IN A UNIVERSE OF CONTINUOUS MOTION

The entire universe is in a state of perpetual motion. From the smallest particles to the largest celestial bodies, nothing in the cosmos remains completely still. There is no such thing as a stationary object when viewed from the broader perspective of space. Whether it is the rotation of planets, the orbiting of moons, or the expansion of galaxies, movement is a fundamental characteristic of the physical universe. This constant motion shapes the very fabric of reality and drives the evolution of everything within it.

Consider the vast scales of motion in our cosmic neighborhood. The Earth itself travels around the Sun at a staggering speed of approximately 107,000 kilometers per hour. Meanwhile, our entire solar system orbits the center of the Milky Way galaxy at around 720,000 kilometers per hour. Even more astonishing is the motion of the Milky Way galaxy itself, which hurtles through space at an estimated velocity of 2.1 million kilometers per hour. Every planet, star, and galaxy is in constant movement, forever occupying new regions of space that they had never been in before. This unending motion is a defining trait of our dynamic universe.

Even on Earth, motion continues on a geologic timescale. The solid ground beneath our feet is not as immobile as it seems. The Earth's crust is made up of tectonic plates that are continuously shifting, albeit slowly, due to the immense forces within the planet. These plates move a few centimeters each year, gradually reshaping continents and ocean floors. Over millions of years, these slow yet powerful movements give rise to mountains, earthquakes, and the drift of continents. This illustrates that motion is not only a cosmic principle but also a crucial process shaping our planet's surface and life itself.

If the entire universe is in perpetual motion, then human beings, as part of that universe, are also subject to continuous change and movement. Just as celestial bodies travel through space without pause, our lives are shaped by constant progression—physically, mentally, and socially. Remaining stagnant is not a natural state, and those who wish to grow must embrace the rhythm of motion that governs the world around us.

We live in a time where intellect has become the most valuable asset. In this age of information and innovation, knowledge drives progress more than any physical resource. Success is no longer solely determined by strength or inheritance, but by the ability to think critically, adapt quickly, and apply what we learn. Those who are committed to advancing in life understand that there is no permanent comfort zone; comfort often leads to complacency, while growth requires stepping into the unknown.

To remain relevant in this fast-paced world, continuous learning is essential. The landscape of technology, science, and society evolves daily, and keeping up demands effort and curiosity. Reading, studying, and exploring new ideas must become habits rather than occasional pursuits. Just as the planets do not pause in their orbits, we too must keep moving—intellectually and personally—if we are to make meaningful progress and find our place in an ever-changing world.

30. ENVIRONMENT MAY DEFINE YOUR PERFORMANCE

In the early days of spring, Pierre eagerly planted a variety of vegetable seeds, taking advantage of the warming soil and lengthening daylight. To his delight, the seeds began to sprout within just a few days, sending up tiny green shoots that signaled the beginning of the growing season. Recognizing the need for more space and sunlight, Pierre carefully transplanted the fragile seedlings from their starter containers into the neatly prepared beds of his vegetable garden, hoping they would thrive in their new environment.

As time passed, many of the transplanted seedlings adapted well to their surroundings and began to grow with remarkable vigor. Their leaves broadened, and their stems strengthened under the nurturing sun and consistent watering. However, not all of the seedlings were as fortunate. Despite Pierre's attentive care, several of them withered and died just a few days after being moved. Whether it was due to transplant shock, pests, or subtle variations in soil conditions, their failure served as a reminder of the delicate balance required in gardening and the unpredictable nature of growing plants from seed.

Companies often base their hiring decisions on a candidate's past experience, using previous roles as indicators of future performance. Resumes, interviews, and reference checks help employers gauge whether a potential employee possesses the skills, knowledge, and work ethic necessary to succeed in the new role. The assumption is that individuals who have performed well in similar positions will continue to do so, especially if the responsibilities and expectations are comparable.

In many cases, this assumption proves true. Most new employees tend to perform in line with how they did at their previous jobs, bringing with them their expertise, habits, and professional mindset. Their familiarity with the tasks and industry often allows for a smoother transition and quicker adaptation. These individuals quickly integrate into their new teams, meet deadlines, and fulfill their responsibilities with minimal supervision, reaffirming the company's decision to hire them based on prior achievements.

However, not all transitions go as smoothly. Some employees may struggle to replicate their previous success, despite having strong resumes and glowing references. This disparity in performance can stem from a variety of factors, such as differences in company culture, team dynamics, or management styles.

A supportive work environment, effective communication with coworkers, and strong leadership are all crucial components that influence an individual's ability to perform well. When these elements are lacking or misaligned with the employee's needs, it can lead to disengagement, stress, and a noticeable decline in productivity. Ultimately, performance is not determined by experience alone but also by the quality of the workplace environment.

31. IDEA FOR HUMANITY'S FIRST HOME

In the earliest days of human civilization, long before cities and technology, our ancestors sought refuge in the natural world. Caves offered protection from the harsh elements— scorching sun, biting winds, torrential rain— and from the dangers posed by wild animals. These rocky shelters served as the first homes, providing safety and a sense of stability in a world governed by survival.

However, as human populations grew and communities began to form, caves became scarce. There simply weren't enough of them to house everyone. People were forced to adapt, seeking alternative forms of shelter in the open landscapes around them.

During oppressive heat or sudden downpours, they would gather under the canopy of trees, relying on nature's umbrella for temporary relief. It was in moments like these that ingenuity sparked. Observing how branches and leaves shielded them from the sky, someone had a simple yet revolutionary idea: "Why not build our own shelter using poles and leaves, like the trees do?"

And so, the concept of the house was born. By erecting wooden poles and covering them with leaves, grass, or animal hides, early humans created the first man-made dwellings—

primitive huts that offered protection and a place to gather, rest, and live. This marked a turning point in human development: the beginning of architecture, and the foundation upon which all future civilizations would rise.

Ideas can emerge from the most unexpected places. Sometimes, a simple walk in nature, the sound of leaves rustling in the breeze, or the gentle rhythm of raindrops on a window can spark a new thought. Even the small challenges we face in daily life—like fixing a broken object or organizing our time better—can inspire creative solutions. When we slow down and take time to observe the world around us, we often discover patterns, problems, or possibilities we hadn't noticed before.

Staying curious is the key. Curiosity fuels the mind to ask questions, seek answers, and explore the unknown. It encourages us to look beyond the surface and dig deeper into how things work or why they are the way they are. Many of history's great thinkers and inventors—like Leonardo da Vinci, Marie Curie, and Thomas Edison—were driven by a deep sense of wonder. Their ability to pay attention to details and ask questions no one else thought to ask led to groundbreaking discoveries.

Once an idea is formed, it becomes the starting point for innovation. With imagination, persistence, and experimentation, that idea can be developed into something practical and impactful. It might take the form of a new tool, a work of art, a scientific theory, or a helpful service. The journey from idea to innovation often involves trial and error, but each step brings us closer to something meaningful. What once began as a simple thought can grow into a powerful force that shapes how we live and interact with the world.

Ultimately, ideas are everywhere—we just need to train ourselves to see them. By cultivating a mindset of curiosity, observation, and open-mindedness, we become more receptive to the sparks of creativity that surround us. Every great invention or advancement began with someone daring to see the world differently. So look around, listen closely, and never stop wondering. The next big idea could be waiting in the most ordinary moment.

32. MODERN THUGS: THE ENDURING PHILOSOPHY OF BETRAYAL

A long time ago in Central India, there was a notorious gang known as the Thugs, who preyed on unsuspecting travelers. They would first befriend their victims, gain their trust by learning about their journey and intentions, and then, once the travelers were distracted and off guard, the Thugs would rob and murder them.

Devin was a hardworking and successful businessman, well-respected in his community for his dedication and integrity. He occasionally hosted guests at his home, enjoying the company of friends and acquaintances. Among these visitors was Julian, someone Devin often welcomed without hesitation. Unknown to Devin, however, Julian was a bitter and envious man who secretly resented anyone more successful than himself. Though he hid his true feelings well, Julian harbored a deep dislike for Devin's prosperity and waited silently for an opportunity to see him fall.

When a severe economic downturn struck, Devin's business began to suffer, pushing him into financial distress. Sensing his vulnerability, an opportunistic office employee filed a false harassment lawsuit in hopes of extracting money. Although the court eventually dismissed the claim due to lack of evidence, the damage to Devin's reputation had already been done. Julian, eager to fan the flames, spread rumors of Devin's troubles throughout the community, tarnishing his image even further. As whispers turned into judgment, Devin found himself alienated and ashamed, unable to face the very society that once admired him. With his reputation shattered and his resources depleted, he sold everything he owned and quietly relocated to a distant town, seeking a fresh start far from the shadows of his ruined past.

In life, we often come across individuals who present themselves as friends, offering a comforting presence and seemingly genuine companionship. They listen to our stories, share in our successes, and earn our trust over time. Believing in their sincerity, we open our hearts to them, revealing personal thoughts, vulnerabilities, and even secrets that we would otherwise guard closely. These relationships feel secure—built on mutual respect and understanding—or so we think.

However, the true nature of some people only emerges when adversity strikes. When our fortunes begin to fade, these so-called friends can transform. Rather than offering support or standing by us in difficult times, they distance themselves—or worse, they become the very ones who spread whispers and doubts about our character. Like vultures circling a wounded animal, they exploit our misfortune, using what they know against us to further their own agendas or elevate their standing. Their loyalty proves hollow, and the friendship, a carefully crafted illusion.

Such betrayals are not new. They echo the cunning of historical figures like the infamous thugs of Central India, who befriended travelers only to rob and murder them once their guard was down. In a similar way, these false friends wear a mask of kindness until the moment it no longer serves them. Their actions remind us to be cautious with our trust, to recognize that not everyone who walks beside us means well, and that true friendship is proven in moments of hardship.

The Thugs themselves may belong to history, yet the philosophy they embodied will endure for all time, resurfacing in subtle and often unexpected ways. Human nature has a tendency to recycle such patterns, and even in modern life, people who appear as friends can sometimes reveal their true colors when adversity strikes. In hardship, masks fall, revealing betrayal and malice that prove treachery endures regardless of the era. We are reminded that while times and faces change, the underlying philosophies of deceit and betrayal remain constant, demanding vigilance, wisdom, and resilience from those who encounter them.

33. BEYOND THE CRUST: THE TRUTH BENEATH THE SURFACE

The exterior of a loaf of bread may vary in shades of brown—ranging from golden to deep, dark crusts—depending on how it was baked, but this outer appearance doesn't necessarily reflect what lies inside. Despite the contrasting outer shell, the interior of most bread remains soft, light, and predominantly white. The crust, though it forms a noticeable first impression, represents only a small fraction of the entire loaf. It's a reminder that outward appearances can be misleading; the true substance, essence, and majority often reside within, hidden beneath the surface and unaffected by external differences.

In a dictatorship, the majority of the population often endures great suffering under rigid and oppressive control. The policies implemented by the regime usually limit basic freedoms, suppress individuality, and enforce strict guidelines on how people must live and work. Citizens are often subjected to harsh punishments for even minor acts of defiance, leaving them with no choice but to comply. Institutions that would normally check the power of a government—such as independent media, judiciary, and civil society—are either dismantled or brought under tight control. In such an environment, fear and silence dominate, and dissent is not only discouraged but actively punished.

Once a dictator has full control over the internal population, they may begin to focus outward. Fueled by unchecked power and a desire for expansion, some regimes attempt to interfere with or even invade neighboring countries. These aggressive moves are often based on the assumption that nearby nations are politically or militarily weaker. However, dictators frequently miscalculate the strength and resilience of these neighbors. The arrogance bred within a dictatorship can lead to strategic blunders, where the regime underestimates its opponents and overestimates its own capabilities.

When cracks begin to appear in the regime's control—whether due to military defeat, economic collapse, or public resistance—the people may rapidly seize the opportunity to overthrow the dictator. Years of silent suffering often boil over into acts of rebellion once the illusion of the dictator's invincibility is broken. A population that has been forced to submit may suddenly unite in defiance, tearing down the very structure that held them captive. In many cases, the downfall of a dictator is swift and dramatic, reflecting how thin and brittle the façade of total control truly was.

34. TEMPTATION TO MAINTAIN THE STATUSQUO

Stan began his journey as a businessman with humble beginnings, working tirelessly to build his fortune and earn a name for himself in the competitive world of commerce. Through determination, grit, and long hours, he climbed the economic ladder and eventually became both wealthy and well-known in social and professional circles. But as his success grew, so did his appetite for luxury and public recognition. The expensive cars, lavish homes, exotic vacations, and high-society events he now considered essential to his image required a steady and increasing flow of money—more than what his legitimate businesses could generate, especially as some of them began to falter and accrue losses.

Driven by the fear of losing status and the desire to maintain his extravagant lifestyle, Stan made the fateful decision to venture into unethical and illegal enterprises. What started as minor infractions escalated into full-fledged illicit operations, including fraudulent accounting, deceptive contracts, and underground deals. For years, he managed to mask these transgressions behind a polished public façade, but the truth eventually caught up with him. After a lengthy investigation, authorities uncovered a web of financial misconduct and deceit, leading to his dramatic arrest. The man once celebrated for his rags-to-riches story became a cautionary tale of how unchecked ambition and moral compromise can bring even the most successful individuals to ruin.

Every human being, no matter how principled or disciplined, faces temptation—especially after tasting success. Whether in business, politics, academics, or any other field, success often brings with it admiration, influence, and a sense of accomplishment. However, it also comes with new pressures: the desire to stay on top, the fear of losing relevance, and the expectations of others. These pressures can subtly invite individuals to cut corners, bend rules, or even cheat in order to maintain their elevated status. The very triumph that was once a source of pride can become a burden, tempting even the most virtuous to compromise their values for the sake of continued glory.

It is important to remember that there is no rule guaranteeing that success is permanent. It is fleeting, and just as easily as one rises, one can fall. The spotlight dims, accolades fade, and competitors arise. Many individuals make the mistake of believing their moment at the top will last forever, only to be blindsided when their influence begins to wane. When that moment of decline arrives—whether through business losses, political unpopularity, or academic setbacks—the true test begins. Will the individual cling to integrity, or will they chase shadows, desperate to reclaim lost prestige by any means necessary? The seductive allure of shortcuts is never stronger than during the decline, when fear and ego can cloud judgment.

Ultimately, it is not success itself that defines a person, but rather how they respond during periods of struggle or obscurity. Lean times, while painful, are opportunities to demonstrate character, humility, and resilience. They offer a chance to rebuild, to reflect on the values that truly matter, and to persevere without compromising one's core principles. Many of history's most respected figures are not remembered solely for their achievements, but for the grace, patience, and moral courage they displayed when fortunes turned. In the grand arc of life, integrity during hardship leaves a deeper legacy than any fleeting moment of triumph won through deceit.

35. JOURNEY FROM POVERTY TO PURPOSE

On a rugged hilltop within a popular national park stands a solitary tree, a striking figure against the sky and stone. This lone tree, defying all odds, has become one of the park's most admired and photographed natural features. Its presence on the harsh, rocky terrain captures the imagination of thousands who visit each year, drawn by the tree's quiet testament to perseverance. Against wind, weather, and the unforgiving stone beneath it, the tree thrives, embodying nature's resilience in the face of adversity.

Many years ago, a single seed was carried—perhaps by wind, bird, or animal—to a narrow crevice in the hill's stony surface. There, it found just enough dust and organic matter to take root. As the sapling grew, its roots slowly dug deeper into the rock, seeking out moisture and nutrients. Over time, the roots expanded and split the stone, creating wider cracks that allowed further growth. Several root branches found neighboring crevices, anchoring the tree even more firmly into the hill. Unlike the other trees in the national park, the lone tree did not have any support during harsh weather conditions. The tree's survival and growth was a slow but powerful act of persistence, as it reshaped the very rock that once seemed inhospitable.

In time, the unusual tree became more than just a natural curiosity—it grew into a symbol of the park itself. Its silhouette is now featured in the park's logo, representing strength, endurance, and harmony with the landscape. Visitors come from far and wide not only to see the tree with their own eyes but also to stand beside it, capturing photographs that reflect its significance.

People are born into various layers of society, each with its own set of opportunities and challenges. Some enter the world into the comfort of wealth, where resources, education, and connections are readily available. Others are born into middle-class families, where stability often comes with hard work and budgeting. Still, many are born into poverty, facing hardships from the very beginning. While these starting points differ greatly, they do not determine a person's worth or potential.

There is a misconception in some circles that being poor is something to be ashamed of. However, this belief overlooks the strength, resilience, and ingenuity that often arise in difficult circumstances. Those raised in poor families frequently learn to stretch every resource, to be creative in solving problems, and to appreciate what they have. Living with less can foster discipline, empathy, and an unshakable drive to improve one's life. Poverty may be a tough beginning, but it can also be a powerful motivator.

It is important to remember that nearly every wealthy family once had humble origins. Somewhere in their lineage, an individual—or several—worked tirelessly to change their family's circumstances. Wealth does not appear overnight; it is often the result of generations of effort, sacrifice, and determination. Being born poor is not shameful—it is simply a starting point. What matters most is not remaining in poverty when the opportunity to rise exists. The real shame is in choosing not to try, not in starting with little.

When a person achieves success, whether financial, professional, or personal, society admires them not just for where they are, but for how far they've come. People are inspired by those who rise above their circumstances, who transform struggle into strength. It's the story of overcoming adversity that resonates—proof that our beginnings do not define our ends. True admiration is earned not by wealth alone, but by the journey taken to attain it.

36. WHEN THE FORTUNE FADES

Young Clara tragically passed away after a brief and sudden illness that left her family in shock and sorrow. As they gathered around her lifeless body, grieving the loss of the bright and gentle child, they were startled to witness an unsettling sight—hair lice emerging and shedding from Clara's hair. The moment, already filled with profound sadness, took on an eerie and haunting quality as the tiny parasites, no longer sensing the warmth and life of their host, began to crawl away in search of survival.

No matter how much kindness, support, or generosity you extend to others, the moment misfortune strikes, many of those who once benefitted from your goodwill begin to fade into the background. These same individuals, who once praised you, dined at your table, and sought your help during their own times of need, may suddenly distance themselves when you fall into hardship. Their smiles vanish, their gratitude disappears, and their true colors begin to show. What once appeared to be friendship or loyalty reveals itself as convenience or opportunism. Some individuals become so emotionally barren, so indifferent to your struggles, that even the frozen fish tucked away in your freezer seems to possess more warmth and compassion than they do.

During times of adversity, you often find yourself alone. The people you assumed would stand by you may act as if they never knew you at all. In your lowest moments, when you most need companionship or a helping hand, there is often no one to turn to. The silence is deafening, and the absence of those you once called friends cuts deeper than the hardship itself. It's a sobering experience to watch familiar faces turn cold and indifferent when your life takes a downward turn.

Yet, misfortune is rarely permanent. Just as the sun returns after the darkest storm, fortune too has a way of circling back. When that moment arrives—when you rise again and regain strength and stability—you will see with clarity the people who truly matter. You will recognize the ones who stayed when it was uncomfortable to do so, who offered comfort without expectation, and who stood by you in quiet solidarity.

This renewed perspective becomes one of the few blessings hardship offers. It teaches discernment and brings wisdom that prosperity alone cannot provide. Going forward, you will hold close those rare souls who stayed true during your trials, and you will no longer be deceived by hollow gestures of friendship. Adversity may isolate you, but it also purifies your circle and helps you rebuild a life rooted in sincerity.

37. REPAIR OR LET GO

Steve worked in real estate, dealing in the buying, selling, and renting of various properties. He had a keen eye for opportunity and often acquired flooded properties at extremely low prices. After making the necessary repairs and renovations, he would resell them at a much higher value, turning a strong profit. His business strategy relied on identifying undervalued assets and transforming them into desirable homes.

On occasion, Steve would take a chance on burned-out properties. While he always hoped to salvage and restore them, more often than not, the damage was too extensive to repair. In such cases, he would have the structure demolished and either sell the land or construct a brand-new house or townhome in its place. His adaptability and willingness to take calculated risks helped him thrive in a competitive market.

Relationships are much like houses in the real estate market. Some are built on solid foundations and, even when damaged, can be repaired with time, effort, and care. Just as a house may suffer from wear and tear but still hold its value with proper renovation, a relationship can go through difficult phases and yet emerge stronger if both parties are willing to invest in restoring it.

However, not all relationships can be salvaged. There are times when the damage is too deep—like a burned-out house where the structure is beyond repair. In such cases, no amount of patching up can bring it back to its original form. The foundation may be cracked, trust may be eroded, or the emotional framework may no longer support the bond.

When that happens, the best choice may be to walk away and start fresh. Just as in real estate, where the land can be cleared to build something new, moving on from a broken relationship opens the door to new beginnings. Letting go doesn't mean failure—it means recognizing what can no longer be fixed and making room for something healthier and more stable to grow.

38. FROM START TO FINISH: PREPARING FOR THE JOURNEY AHEAD

Jamie was a newspaper reporter whose office was located in the heart of the city. Every morning, he followed a strict routine, leaving his house around 7:00 AM to catch the 7:30 AM train. Punctual and reliable, the train was a crucial part of his daily commute, allowing him to navigate the long distance between his suburban neighborhood and the bustling city center.

The train itself began its journey from a far-off southern city at 5:00 AM, steadily making its way northward with precise timing. By the time Jamie boarded, it was well into its route. After a peaceful ride filled with quiet reflection or last-minute edits to his articles, he would arrive at his office by 9:00 AM, ready to chase the day's stories and meet looming deadlines.

Every journey in education or any meaningful project begins with a clear start date. This moment marks the beginning of a commitment—an entry into a period of learning, growth, and discipline. Whether it's the first day of school, the launch of a research project, or the start of a personal goal, it signifies the opening of a chapter filled with opportunities and challenges. This initial phase often comes with excitement, hope, and sometimes uncertainty, but it lays the foundation for everything that follows.

As with all things, there is also an end date—a final deadline, an exam, a presentation, or a moment of evaluation. That end point may feel distant at the beginning, but it is always approaching, whether you're ready or not. Time moves steadily forward, and the pressure of the finish line can either serve as a motivator or a source of stress. That's why it's crucial to stay focused, manage time wisely, and consistently put in effort throughout the process. Procrastination only makes the final stretch harder, while steady preparation eases the burden and builds confidence.

In the end, the results often reflect the quality of the journey. Those who prepare diligently, make use of available resources, and remain committed to the goal tend to reach the finish line not only successfully but also with a sense of fulfillment. Education and projects aren't just about meeting deadlines—they're about personal growth, acquiring skills, and building resilience. The end date isn't something to fear, but rather a milestone to work toward with purpose and dedication.

39. VISION

Phill arrived at a sprawling office complex located in the quiet suburbs to meet with a client. His first appointment was with an officer whose office was situated on the sixth floor of the building. As he stepped inside, Phill was struck by the panoramic view through the wide windows. The office overlooked an expansive, meticulously manicured lawn that stretched out gracefully below. At the center of the lawn, a serene pond reflected the sky, bordered by a winding walkway that curved through the greenery. Along the edges, flowering trees added bursts of color to the scene, their blossoms swaying gently in the breeze, creating a peaceful and picturesque atmosphere that contrasted with the formality of the business meeting.

Following the initial discussion, Phill proceeded to his next appointment on the second floor. However, the view from this office was markedly different. When he glanced out the window, hoping for another look at the scenic landscape, his line of sight was blocked by dense shrubbery and small trees planted close to the building. The foliage, while well-kept, obscured any view of the lawn, pond, or flowering trees beyond. What had been a wide, open vista just minutes before was now reduced to a green barrier, cutting him off from the tranquility he had admired earlier.

Though we may share the same family roots, attend the same college, or grow up in the same neighborhood, each of us carries a unique lens through which we view the world. Our experiences, upbringing, and personal circumstances shape our perceptions in ways that are often subtle but profound. Even something as basic as our physical differences—like height or eyesight—can influence how we interpret a situation. Add to that our levels of education, life philosophies, and deeply held values, and it becomes clear that no two people truly see the world in the same way, even when standing side by side.

Perspective is also shaped by our roles in society. A businessman, for example, may walk into a community and see opportunities for development, investment, or profit. He may evaluate things based on cost, potential revenue, or market reach. In contrast, a person working for a non-profit might look at the same space and see a chance to serve underprivileged communities, preserve the environment, or uplift lives. Their definitions of success, value, and impact are built on entirely different foundations, even if they are observing the same physical reality.

Similarly, morality and intent can further alter perception. A thief might see a valuable item and immediately think of how to steal it for personal gain. To him, it's a means to an end. Meanwhile, a priest or community leader could look at the very same item and view it as something that could be used to benefit the public—perhaps as a tool for teaching, worship, or charity. What we see is not just shaped by the eyes we look through, but by the hearts and minds behind them. This divergence in perspective reminds us to be humble in our judgments and open to the ways others interpret the world around them.

40. WHEN PASSION OUTPACES PRACTICALITY

Jeff had always been passionate about cars—perhaps "passionate" was too mild a word. Cars were his obsession. He devoured every car magazine he could find, memorizing engine specs, horsepower ratings, and design changes from year to year. Whenever there was a car race nearby, Jeff would be there, cheering on the drivers and studying every move they made. He never missed an auto show, and even on weekends with no events, he would wander through car dealerships, talking to salespeople about the latest models and imagining himself behind the wheel. He was always up to date with the latest trends in the automotive world, from cutting-edge technology to the smallest design details.

When it came to his own vehicle, Jeff spared no expense. He wanted it to be more than just a means of transportation—he wanted it to be a statement. His car had plush, custom-made seats that seemed to hug the driver and passengers in comfort. The audio system was top-of-the-line, equipped with surround sound speakers that made every song feel like a live concert. Lights illuminated the interior in a range of colors, and external lighting gave his car a glow that turned heads on the street. From specialized rims to rare accessories,

Jeff's car was an extension of his personality: bold, flashy, and meticulously maintained.

But as the odometer crept toward 175,000 miles, the glory days began to fade. The once-reliable car started developing problems—first small issues, then costly repairs. It seemed as if every few weeks Jeff was back at the workshop, signing off on another bill that drained his wallet. No matter how much he had invested in luxury features, the reality was that the mechanical components were aging, and keeping the car running smoothly was becoming a losing battle.

Eventually, Jeff decided it was time to part ways with his beloved machine. He expected that all the high-end accessories and modifications would add value, but he was in for a rude awakening. The offers he received were shockingly low. He tried every platform he could—online marketplaces, car forums, local ads—but the results were always the same. Potential buyers cared far more about the car's age, mileage, and mechanical condition than about custom seats or mood lighting. Reluctantly, Jeff sold the car for a fraction of what he had hoped, realizing he had little choice if he wanted to stop pouring money into repairs.

Looking back, Jeff understood an important lesson: whether it's a car, a house, or even an office space, excessive customization and luxury upgrades don't guarantee long-term value. The market rarely rewards personal touches that appeal only to the owner, and years later, those additions often become irrelevant—or even a burden. Practicality and maintenance matter far more in the long run than extravagant details. While Jeff still loved cars, his next vehicle would be chosen with both passion and practicality in mind, balancing his enthusiasm with a dose of financial wisdom.

41. THE WEIGHT OF UNFULFILLED DUTY

Late one night, a thief set his sights on a palatial house that was heavily fenced and guarded. As he waited for the right moment to sneak inside, he spotted two Doberman dogs patrolling the grounds. Realizing there was no chance of slipping past them, he turned his attention to the neighboring, much smaller house. There, he noticed a painter's ladder leaning against a wall. Using it to climb onto the roof and then into a small window, he managed to gain entry. Inside, he found two small dogs—a Pomeranian and a Dachshund. Unlike the Dobermans, these pets were confused but harmless, offering no resistance as the thief searched through the rooms. He quickly gathered valuables, stuffing them into a large bag, and made his way toward the kitchen door exit.

Before leaving, thirst overcame him, and he ventured into the kitchen. Opening the refrigerator, he found a bottle of juice to drink and some meat, which he kindly shared with the two little dogs that had followed him. But when he opened the kitchen door, he was startled to see the two Dobermans from the palatial house glaring at him. Thinking quickly, the thief grabbed more meat from the refrigerator, feeding some directly to the dogs to calm them. He then placed extra meat on the kitchen floor. As the Dobermans entered to eat, he slipped out and slammed the door shut behind them, trapping the guard dogs inside while he fled the scene with his loot.

Weeks later, the thief was caught by police for trespassing and, under questioning, confessed to the break-in at the palatial house. When he was brought before the owner, Mr. Joseph, he admitted that he had fed the guard dogs meat from the refrigerator that night. Mr. Joseph's face grew pale as he heard the details. He revealed that after the burglary, he had scolded the Dobermans harshly for failing in their duty, believing they had simply allowed the thief to escape. Feeling guilty and ashamed, the loyal dogs refused to eat and died of starvation within a week. The tragic story is true.

Sometimes in life, we are faced with responsibilities that demand our full attention and effort. Yet, despite our best intentions, there are moments when we fall short and fail in our duty. Such failures may not always stem from laziness or neglect, but rather from circumstances beyond our control, misjudgments, or simple human weakness. Still, the realization that we did not meet the expectations placed upon us—whether by others, by society, or by ourselves—can weigh heavily on the heart. The sense of having disappointed someone or let an important task slip can leave a lasting scar that is difficult to erase.

Living with guilt becomes an inevitable part of that failure. It lingers quietly, reminding us of what could have been done differently. While guilt can be painful, it also has the power to transform us, teaching humility, compassion, and the importance of vigilance in our responsibilities. The challenge lies not in avoiding mistakes altogether, but in accepting them with honesty and using them as stepping stones toward becoming stronger and more dependable. In this way, even our moments of failure can serve as teachers, guiding us toward a life of deeper responsibility and wisdom.

42. A GOOD WORKER HAS A GREAT OUTLOOK ON LIFE

A good worker maintains a positive outlook on life, approaching every task with dedication and enthusiasm. Regardless of the challenges or obstacles that arise, he remains committed to giving his best effort. His determination and resilience allow him to stay focused, ensuring that his work is completed with excellence. He does not allow negativity or difficulties to deter him; instead, he views every challenge as an opportunity for growth. His optimism and work ethic set him apart, making him a valuable asset in any environment.

Beyond personal success, a good worker positively influences those around him. His dedication and strong work ethic inspire his colleagues, encouraging them to strive for excellence as well. Whether in an office, a factory, or a hospital, his commitment to quality work fosters a culture of responsibility and motivation. His attitude creates a ripple effect, leading to improved teamwork, productivity, and morale. He understands that his efforts do not go unnoticed and that his enthusiasm can uplift those who may feel discouraged or unmotivated.

On a larger scale, the impact of a good worker extends beyond his immediate surroundings and contributes to the development of society as a whole. When individuals take pride in their work and perform their duties with diligence, they help strengthen industries, boost the economy, and enhance the quality of life for their communities. Their efforts lead to innovation, progress, and a more stable and prosperous nation. A society built on hardworking and dedicated individuals thrives because each person plays a role in driving positive change. Ultimately, a good worker is not just someone who completes tasks efficiently but someone whose work leaves a lasting mark on those around him and the world at large.

43. ONCE A STAR, NOW A BLACK DWARF

Once, they were the brightest stars—students who stood out in school and college, impressing everyone with their academic achievements and potential. Teachers, peers, and even family members had high hopes for their futures, believing they would rise to become leaders, innovators, or experts who would make significant contributions to society. Their intelligence and ambition set them apart, and it seemed like they were destined for greatness. However, as time goes on, many of these promising individuals fail to live up to the expectations. Instead of shining brightly, they slowly fade, becoming what one might call "black dwarfs." This transformation is a mystery to those who once admired them, and it leaves many people wondering, "What happened?"

The downfall of these once-promising stars often begins when they face their first real failure or setback. Throughout their youth, they may have breezed through school, effortlessly acing tests and assignments. Their natural intelligence carried them through many challenges without much struggle. However, as they enter the real world, they encounter situations where raw academic knowledge isn't enough to succeed. A single failure, whether it's a missed opportunity, a career misstep, or a personal setback, can shake their confidence and interest in continuing their pursuit of excellence. Unable to cope with this failure, some of these former stars lose the motivation to move forward, and the spark they once had begins to flicker out.

While these individuals may have amassed a great deal of theoretical knowledge, they often lack the practical skills needed to succeed in the real world. Being able to memorize facts and solve problems on paper is one thing, but the ability to apply that knowledge effectively in everyday life is another. Many of these bright minds struggle to navigate the complexities of the workplace, relationships, and the challenges that come with adulthood. Without hands-on experience or the ability to adapt to real-world situations, their academic achievements alone are not enough to sustain their success.

Another key issue with these former stars is their lack of empathy. They tend to focus on their own abilities and achievements, often comparing themselves to others in unhealthy ways. When they see someone else excel, they may feel threatened or envious, rather than inspired. This inability to empathize with others can create a sense of isolation, as they struggle to connect with those around them. They may view the success of others as a reflection of their own inadequacies, rather than recognizing it as a natural part of life. This mindset can lead to frustration, resentment, and ultimately, a reluctance to engage with people who they perceive as competition.

The once-promising students often fall into arrogance, lacking humility, which ultimately causes their downfall. Their early success and sharp intellect lead them to believe they are superior to others, making them dismissive of collaboration and personal growth. This arrogance blinds them to their own shortcomings and the lessons they could learn from failure. Without the ability to recognize their flaws or adapt to challenges, their pride isolates them from those around them, stalling their progress. Additionally, these individuals often lack essential social skills, having focused so much on academics that they neglected emotional intelligence, teamwork, and effective communication. This gap in their development makes it difficult for others to connect with or work alongside them. They may refuse to engage with anyone they deem "lesser mortals," instead surrounding themselves with those who share their intellectual caliber, which limits their opportunities for growth. In the end, the very qualities that once set them apart—intelligence, ambition, and drive—become their greatest weaknesses when not balanced with humility, empathy, and social awareness.

44. BEHIND THE VEIL

After spending many years surrounded by the towering buildings and bustling streets of the city, Roger finally moved to a quiet suburban neighborhood, eager for a change of pace. His new home boasted a spacious backyard filled with tall, mature trees that added a sense of tranquility and natural beauty to the landscape. He loved waking up to the sight of lush greenery and the sound of birds chirping, a stark contrast to the concrete jungle he had left behind. However, as winter arrived and the temperatures dropped, he noticed a dramatic transformation—every tree in his yard shed its leaves, leaving behind bare, skeletal branches. The once-dense foliage that had provided privacy and a sense of seclusion was now gone, revealing a clear view of the neighboring houses beyond.

Wealth and fame draw many close, but only loss reveals who truly cares. Wealth and fame have a way of attracting people, often drawing in friends, admirers, and even distant relatives who suddenly seem eager to be a part of your life. When you are successful, people surround you, offering their friendship, support, and constant attention. They shower you with praise, laugh at your jokes, and always seem to have time for you. However, beneath the surface, it can be difficult to tell who truly values you as a person and who is simply drawn to the advantages that come with your status. The comfort and excitement of being admired can sometimes cloud your judgment, making it easy to believe that the friendships and relationships you have built will always remain strong.

However, the true test of any relationship comes when wealth and fame begin to fade. The moment financial troubles arise or public attention shifts away, the crowd that once surrounded you begins to thin. Friends who once called every day may become too busy, invitations to lavish gatherings may stop arriving, and the warmth of admiration turns into distant politeness or even indifference. This sudden change can be a painful realization, forcing you to confront the uncomfortable truth that many of those who seemed closest to you were not there for your personality, values, or kindness, but for the benefits that came with knowing you.

Yet, within this harsh reality lies a valuable lesson. When all material advantages disappear, the people who remain by your side—those who check on you, offer their support without expecting anything in return, and stand with you in difficult times—are the ones who truly care. It is only in moments of loss and hardship that you can truly see the depth of someone's loyalty and love. While it may be disheartening to lose those who were only there for your wealth, the clarity that comes with such experiences allows you to cherish the rare and genuine relationships that were never built on material gain, but on true affection and loyalty.

45. NOT OUR BATTLE, YET OUR FIGHT

In the vast African savanna, a lively sparrow developed an unusual friendship with a colony of ants living beneath an old, towering tree. Every day, the sparrow would return from its flights across the grasslands and share stories of the world beyond the ants' underground home. The ants, fascinated by the grand tales of mighty beasts and fierce battles, gathered eagerly to listen. The sparrow spoke of towering elephants, swift cheetahs, and dramatic encounters between hunters and prey, painting vivid pictures with its words.

One day, the sparrow brought news of a fierce battle between a pride of lions and a powerful Cape buffalo. The lions, cunning and relentless, sought to bring down the massive beast, while the buffalo, strong and determined, fought back with all its might. The ants, though small and far removed from the actual battle, became deeply invested in the story. They began to take sides—some cheered for the lions, admiring their teamwork and strategy, while others rooted for the buffalo, impressed by its resilience and strength. What started as a friendly discussion among the ants soon turned into heated arguments, each group fiercely defending its chosen side.

As time went on, these debates grew more intense. The sparrow continued to bring colorful reports from the savanna—sometimes the lions triumphed, and other times the Cape buffalo emerged victorious. With each new tale, the ants' discussions became more passionate. Eventually, some arguments escalated into outright fights, with ants turning against their own kin over creatures they had never seen and battles they had never witnessed firsthand. The sparrow, amused by the chaos it had unknowingly sparked, continued sharing its stories, unaware of how deeply they were affecting the ants.

This peculiar behavior among the ants mirrors what often happens among people in the modern world. In social media and friendship circles, discussions about distant events—battles, politics, or controversies in faraway lands—often lead to heated debates. People, despite having no direct connection to the events, take passionate stances and sometimes even argue aggressively. The intensity of these debates can strain relationships, just as it did among the ants, proving that even when an issue has no immediate impact on one's life, emotions can still run high.

In the end, the tale of the sparrow and the ants serves as a reminder of how stories—whether from a tiny bird in the savanna or a news report on social media—can shape opinions, spark conflicts, and stir deep emotions. While engaging in discussions about the world is natural and important, it is equally essential to remember the value of perspective and understanding. Just as the ants allowed distant events to create division among them, people must be mindful of how they engage with stories from afar, ensuring that their debates lead to insight rather than unnecessary discord.

46. THE FOUNDATION OF INDUSTRY: THE ROLE OF PIONEERING OCCUPATIONS

Pioneering occupations, such as farming, fishing, writing, woodcutting, mining, and scientific research, play a fundamental role in the development of industries. These professionals are the backbone of various economic sectors, laying the groundwork for production, trade, and technological advancements. These pioneering occupations provide the drive for industries and economy of countries. Farmers provide the raw materials for the food and textile industries, fishermen supply seafood markets, and authors contribute to education and entertainment. Similarly, woodcutters supply timber for construction and paper manufacturing, miners extract essential minerals for industrial use, and scientists push the boundaries of innovation, leading to new discoveries and advancements. Without these pioneers, the industries that rely on their contributions would not be able to thrive.

While these occupations are crucial, they often come with challenges, including physically demanding labor, financial instability, and unpredictable conditions. Farmers and fishermen, for example, are heavily dependent on weather patterns, while woodcutters and miners face hazardous working environments. Authors and scientists may struggle for recognition and funding, as their work often requires years of dedication before yielding significant results. Despite these obstacles, those engaged in pioneering jobs take the first step in driving economic growth. Their efforts set in motion the production and supply chains that sustain industries such as food processing, publishing, construction, manufacturing, and scientific development.

At the foundational level, pioneering workers may receive modest pay due to the direct and labor-intensive nature of their work. However, as one moves up the job hierarchy, remuneration tends to increase. For instance, a farmer working independently might earn less than an agricultural business owner who manages large-scale operations. Similarly, a miner extracting raw materials earns less than an industrial executive overseeing a mining corporation. Scientists who start with basic research may later achieve high salaries in specialized fields or through patents and innovations. Thus, while pioneering occupations require perseverance and dedication, they serve as stepping stones to higher economic success, benefiting both individuals and society as a whole.

47. FOLLOWING THE MOVING TRAFFIC LIGHT

Every vehicle is equipped with signal lights at the rear, primarily designed to communicate the driver's intended movements to those behind. These lights serve as a crucial safety mechanism, allowing the driver behind to anticipate whether the vehicle in front will slow down, stop, or make a turn. When the brake lights glow red, it signals the driver to slow down or stop, preventing potential rear-end collisions. Similarly, turn signals indicate whether the vehicle intends to change lanes or make a turn, enabling smoother traffic flow. Without these signals, misunderstandings and misjudgments can occur, resulting in chaos— much like a sudden stop without brake lights could cause an accident.

Trade and scientific journals, as well as magazines, serve as valuable sources of information, offering insights into the latest advancements, innovations, and breakthroughs in various fields. These publications are specifically tailored for professionals, researchers, and industry experts, providing them with up-to-date knowledge about cutting-edge technologies, discoveries, and best practices. Whether it is a new development in medical research, a breakthrough in engineering, or an innovative business strategy, these journals act as a bridge between emerging knowledge and practical application. By consistently reading such publications, individuals can stay informed about ongoing trends and remain competitive in their respective fields.

For professionals, staying updated through these journals is not merely a matter of curiosity but a necessity for growth and relevance. For instance, a physician who regularly reads medical journals gains insights into new treatment protocols, emerging drugs, or groundbreaking diagnostic tools, which can significantly improve patient care. Likewise, a civil engineer who follows industry publications stays informed about modern construction materials, sustainable designs, and efficient project management practices, allowing them to implement the latest methodologies in their work. Similarly, a business leader reading trade journals can anticipate market shifts, evolving customer preferences, and innovative business strategies, enabling them to stay ahead of their competition. Thus, these journals not only expand knowledge but also enhance the quality of work delivered by professionals.

Furthermore, these publications often provide a glimpse into the future of industries and professions by highlighting upcoming technologies, potential market disruptions, and shifts in consumer behavior. Early awareness of such changes can give individuals and businesses a competitive edge by allowing them to adapt or innovate before their peers. For example, in the technology sector, journals often publish information about emerging fields such as artificial intelligence, quantum computing, and biotechnology, enabling professionals to align their skills accordingly. In the agriculture sector, trade magazines offer insights into sustainable farming practices, new crop protection methods, and market demand trends, helping farmers optimize their yield and profitability. Ultimately, investing time in reading these journals equips individuals with knowledge, foresight, and strategic acumen, fostering both personal and professional advancement.

48. OBEYING AND SEEKING GUIDANCE FROM THE MENTOR

Stephy had high hopes of living a luxurious and carefree life when she married Paul, a successful business tycoon. She envisioned a life filled with grand parties, exotic vacations, and the privilege of living in a well-established business family. However, Paul's mother, Grace, who had managed the household and played a significant role in supporting Paul's business endeavors, had a different perspective. Grace took it upon herself to mentor Stephy, believing that a well-run household and a supportive wife were crucial for maintaining the stability of a business family. She patiently taught Stephy the nuances of managing the home, understanding the business culture, and maintaining harmony within the family. However, Stephy did not appreciate her mother-in-law's guidance and often viewed it as unnecessary preaching. Instead of embracing the wisdom that Grace offered, Stephy would occasionally leave Paul's house to stay at her parental home, finding temporary solace from the responsibilities that came with being the wife of a business tycoon.

Time passed, and unexpectedly, Grace passed away, leaving a void in the household. With her mother-in-law gone, Stephy assumed she would finally live a life of leisure and luxury without any interference. However, reality struck differently. Without Grace's guidance, Stephy found it extremely difficult to manage the household, handle social gatherings, and support Paul in his business affairs. The discipline and organizational structure that Grace had carefully built began to crumble under Stephy's watch. Simple tasks such as managing domestic staff, overseeing house operations, and hosting dignitaries soon became overwhelming for her. Paul, who relied heavily on his mother's support in maintaining order in the family, noticed the gradual deterioration of their home's atmosphere. Stephy realized too late the value of Grace's mentorship, but by then, the chaos had already set in. What could have been a seamless and luxurious life turned into a stressful and disordered existence, simply because Stephy disregarded the lessons that could have made her a strong pillar in her family.

Working with experienced personnel can sometimes feel tiresome, especially for those who are new to a profession or field. Seasoned individuals often carry a wealth of knowledge gathered from years of practical experience, failures, and successes. They have faced challenges, solved complex problems, and developed unique insights that cannot be found in textbooks or training manuals. When these experienced individuals work alongside younger or less experienced counterparts, they instinctively take on the role of mentors, sharing their wisdom and offering guidance. However, their approach may sometimes come across as repetitive or outdated to the newer generation, leading to a lack of interest or appreciation for the knowledge being imparted. Many people tend to overlook the value of such experience until it is too late, failing to realize that the knowledge gained through years of hands-on practice is irreplaceable.

The true importance of learning from experienced individuals only becomes evident when they are no longer around. Once they pass away or retire, their practical knowledge, unique problem-solving abilities, and valuable insights disappear with them, leaving a void that can never be filled. It is often then that people realize how much could have been learned if only they had paid closer attention. The lessons that once seemed monotonous or unnecessary turn out to be crucial for handling real-world challenges. For example, an experienced craftsman can teach the finer nuances of his trade — something that a textbook or online tutorial can never fully capture. Similarly, a senior business executive who has weathered economic downturns and market crashes can offer invaluable strategies for survival and growth. However, when such individuals are gone, the newer generation is often left struggling to figure things out on their own, regretting the missed opportunity to learn from those who had already walked the path.

It is therefore essential to approach working with experienced personnel with humility, curiosity, and a genuine desire to learn. Instead of viewing their constant guidance as a burden, one must recognize it as an opportunity to gain knowledge that can significantly shape their own professional growth. Asking questions, observing their methods, and understanding the reasoning behind their decisions can provide invaluable insights that no formal education can offer. Time is often limited, and the wisdom of experienced individuals is like a treasure chest — once lost, it can never be recovered. Thus, it is wise to absorb as much knowledge as possible while they are still present, rather than waiting until it is too late and being left with regret. By embracing their mentorship, individuals not only accelerate their learning curve but also ensure the preservation and continuation of practical knowledge that has stood the test of time.

49. WHITEWASHING

Clement was shocked to discover that his house had been vandalized. Someone had used crayons to scrawl a large, colorful drawing across one of the exterior walls. Though annoyed, he quickly took action, applying several coats of fresh paint to cover the markings. After careful effort, the crayon artwork was completely concealed, and his house was restored to its former appearance.

Months later, however, Clement faced an even bigger problem. This time, his house had been defaced with graffiti—bold, black paint sprayed across the same wall. Determined to erase the damage, he once again picked up his paintbrush and covered the graffiti with multiple layers of paint. Yet, no matter how many coats he applied, the dark, stubborn marks bled through, refusing to be hidden.

When a member of a family commits a wrongdoing, there is often a natural instinct among other members to conceal it in order to avoid shame or embarrassment. Whether it is a small mistake or a significant transgression, families may go to great lengths to cover up the issue, believing that by doing so, they are protecting their reputation and preserving harmony within the household. They might offer excuses, downplay the severity of the offense, or even remain silent in the hope that the matter will fade away with time.

However, if the wrongdoing continues, it becomes increasingly difficult to keep it hidden. Patterns of behavior have a way of resurfacing, no matter how much effort is made to suppress them. What was once a private matter may begin to manifest in unexpected ways— through whispers in the community, strained relationships, or visible consequences that can no longer be ignored. The more a family tries to mask the issue, the more evident it becomes, much like a stain that refuses to disappear despite repeated attempts to cover it.

In the end, avoiding the truth only delays the inevitable. When problems go unaddressed, they often grow worse, affecting not only the individual responsible but also the entire family. True resolution comes not from concealment but from acknowledgment and accountability. By facing the issue head-on and seeking a solution, families can prevent further damage and foster a healthier, more honest environment where mistakes are seen as opportunities for growth rather than sources of lasting shame.

50. NEVER LOSE THE GRIP

James had built the house with his own hands—every brick, every nail, every beam held a piece of his soul. It was meant to be a sanctuary for his wife, Laura, and their two children, Ethan and Lily, a place where love and laughter would always fill the rooms. For years, life was good. James ran a modest carpentry business, crafting furniture with precision and care, while Laura, an artist, painted murals that brightened schools and community centers. Their home smelled of freshly baked bread and echoed with bedtime stories. But when the economy took a downturn, James's business suffered. Fewer people sought handcrafted furniture, and bills began piling up. Soon, foreclosure loomed over them like a storm cloud, replacing warmth with tension, whispers, and quiet, worried glances.

One evening, as James sat on the creaking porch steps, Ethan approached him with his skateboard. "Remember when you fixed this for me?" he asked. That memory sparked an idea. Instead of making new furniture, James could repair what people already had. The next day, he put up a sign: **Carter's Repair – We Fix What Matters.** At first, it was small jobs—mending broken chairs, restoring cabinets—but word spread quickly. A boutique owner noticed his craftsmanship and commissioned him for more work. Laura painted designs on refurbished pieces, and even Ethan and Lily pitched in. The family found joy again, not just in saving their home, but in working together. As James stood on the porch one evening, watching his family laugh, he realized it wasn't the house that had saved them—it was the love they had poured into it. They had never truly lost their grip. They had just needed to find a new way to hold on.

There are moments in life when everything feels like it's slipping away—your business, your family, the very foundation you worked so hard to build. The walls that once stood strong start to tremble under the weight of hardship, and no matter how much effort you put in, it seems like you're fighting a losing battle. The late nights filled with worry, the arguments fueled by stress, and the lingering doubt in your mind whisper that you're on the brink of losing everything. The dreams you built with love and dedication feel fragile, and fear creeps in, making you wonder if all your work was in vain. It's in these moments of despair that you are truly tested—not just by circumstances, but by your ability to hold on, to adapt, and to believe that things can change.

But even in the darkest moments, perseverance, love, and hope have a way of pushing through. The hard work you put in does not disappear; it builds silently, waiting for the right moment to shine. Sometimes, the path forward isn't what you originally envisioned, but rather a new opportunity hidden in the rubble of your struggles. When you refuse to give up, when you find another way to fight for what matters, the tide begins to turn. A small spark—a fresh idea, a helping hand, a moment of clarity—can reignite everything you thought was lost. In the end, it's not just your business or your home that is saved, but the bonds that hold your family together. No matter how shaky the foundation may seem, love, resilience, and determination will always find a way to rebuild and strengthen it.

51. THIEF AND THE POLICE

The concept of police and security emerged as a direct response to theft. In early human societies, as people began to settle into more permanent communities and engage in agriculture, the accumulation of goods became more common. With this increase in wealth, there was a rise in theft, as individuals sought to take what wasn't theirs, particularly food and household items. To protect these valuable possessions, early forms of policing and security were created, often in the form of community-based watch systems or appointed guards to deter or respond to theft.

In this sense, theft predates formal policing, as it is a behavior rooted in basic human instincts and societal dynamics. The need for protection against theft, however, prompted the establishment of law enforcement structures, which were designed to maintain order and safeguard property. Over time, these security measures evolved into more organized systems of policing, creating the modern law enforcement institutions we recognize today.

In today's fast-paced world, false news tends to spread much more rapidly than the truth. This phenomenon is often driven by sensationalism and the desire to capture attention, with individuals and media outlets rushing to publish stories without verifying their accuracy. Social media platforms and news outlets can amplify these falsehoods, creating an environment where misinformation spreads like wildfire. The allure of a compelling story, whether based on speculation or outright fabrication, can overshadow the cautious, fact-checking process required to ensure the truth is fully understood. As a result, many people believe the first version of events they hear, even if it's not entirely accurate.

However, the truth, though it may be slower to emerge, ultimately prevails. It requires more time and careful investigation to uncover, as facts are often buried under layers of distortion. The process of verifying sources, cross-checking details, and conducting thorough research ensures that accurate information surfaces, though it may take longer than the initial rush of misinformation. Therefore, it is essential to remain cautious and keep an open mind when encountering news. Always take a moment to critically evaluate the information you receive, and remember that the truth will eventually come to light, even if it takes time. By being mindful and patient, you can better navigate the flood of news and arrive at a more informed understanding of events.

52. COLLIDING WITH TRUTH

Martin, a dedicated and innovative cashier at a prominent city bank, had earned a reputation for his diligence and forward-thinking approach. His managers recognized his contributions and had scheduled him for a well-deserved promotion. However, not everyone at the bank shared in the excitement over Martin's success. Lawrence, a fellow employee known for his subpar performance and questionable work ethics, also applied for the same promotion. Envious of Martin's achievements, Lawrence grew bitter when he realized he was unlikely to be selected due to his poor track record.

Driven by jealousy, Lawrence devised a malicious scheme to sabotage Martin's career. Enlisting the help of his accomplice Gonzalves, a clerk at the bank, Lawrence secretly hid a large sum of money in a vault section under Martin's responsibility. When the missing funds were discovered during a routine audit, all evidence pointed toward Martin, who was promptly suspended from his position. The news of his suspension spread quickly throughout his community, leaving Martin heartbroken and in disbelief. Isolated and shamed, he withdrew from public life, consumed by despair and confusion over the betrayal.

Fate took a turn when Martin's loyal friend, Gomez, overheard a drunken conversation at a local bar where Lawrence and Gonzalves bragged about their deceit. Wasting no time, Gomez rushed to inform Martin. Together, they alerted the authorities, leading to a police investigation that uncovered the hidden money in an abandoned building. The evidence confirmed Martin's innocence, and Lawrence and Gonzalves were arrested for their crimes. Martin was reinstated at the bank with honors and finally received the promotion he had earned. The community, once saddened by the injustice he faced, now celebrated his vindication and return, rallying around him with pride and support.

False news spreads like a whirlwind, swirling through conversations, headlines, and social media with astonishing speed. Lies, by their very nature, are designed to capture attention—they are often dramatic, sensational, and emotionally charged, making them easy to believe and even easier to share. Much like a sprinter at the starting line, a lie bolts into the public consciousness, gaining traction before anyone has a chance to question its validity. People pass it along without pause, caught in the rush of shock or excitement, unaware of the damage it leaves in its wake.

In contrast, truth is slow and deliberate. It takes time to uncover facts, verify sources, and sift through misinformation. Truth, like a careful runner tying their shoelaces before beginning a marathon, requires patience and persistence. It doesn't compete in the race for attention but instead moves steadily forward, grounded in integrity and reason. The process may be long and often frustrating, as lies continue to spread unchecked, but truth never falters. It walks confidently, knowing that its strength lies not in speed but in endurance and clarity.

Eventually, the paths of lies and truth intersect, and when they do, lies cannot withstand the weight of evidence and reality. The truth exposes deceit, unravels false narratives, and brings justice and clarity to what was once obscured. Though lies may dominate the beginning of the story, truth inevitably claims the final word. In the end, it is truth that endures, heals, and restores trust. No matter how far or fast lies may travel, truth always catches up—and when it does, it triumphs, unequivocally and eternally.

53. HAPPINESS TUNES US

Marco had been eagerly anticipating the release of a particular comedy movie for quite some time, and when it finally hit theaters, he wasted no time in getting a ticket. The cinema was packed with excited moviegoers, and Marco found himself seated in the middle row, surrounded on all sides. As the film began, laughter erupted throughout the theater, with the audience enjoying every comedic moment. However, about halfway through the movie, Marco suddenly felt the urgent need to use the restroom. Not wanting to inconvenience those around him by squeezing past them in the dark, he decided to wait it out and stay in his seat until the end of the film.

Despite his initial excitement, Marco found it nearly impossible to focus on the movie from that point forward. The discomfort distracted him completely, and the urge to leave kept growing stronger with every passing minute. While the rest of the audience roared with laughter at the film's funniest scenes, Marco sat in silence, unable to enjoy the humor that had once drawn him there. What was supposed to be a joyful experience turned into a tense waiting game, leaving him feeling frustrated and disappointed by the time the credits rolled.

Our enjoyment of music, movies, and other forms of entertainment is deeply tied to our emotional well-being. When we are happy, we are more open to the pleasures these experiences offer. A cheerful mood heightens our senses and allows us to laugh freely at a witty scene, feel moved by a powerful melody, or relate deeply to the emotions of a character on screen. In such moments, entertainment becomes more than just a pastime—it becomes a celebration of our joy, amplifying our positive emotions and offering a shared sense of connection and delight. We find meaning and beauty more readily because our hearts are in tune with the content we are experiencing.

However, when our emotional state shifts—whether due to sadness, depression, or anxiety—the same experiences can feel dull or meaningless. Nervousness, in particular, can be just as paralyzing to our ability to enjoy as sadness. Even in luxurious settings, such as five-star hotels or premium flights often arranged by companies for high-stakes business meetings, the mental burden of impending decisions and performance expectations can weigh heavily. Employees in such situations may feel too anxious to appreciate the comfort and elegance around them. Similarly, in times of sadness or depression, our emotional lens distorts our perception, turning vibrant films and uplifting songs into hollow echoes. The mind becomes consumed by its internal struggles, cutting us off from sources of joy that once felt effortless. It's not the external world that has dimmed, but our ability to connect with it that has been clouded by emotional weight.

54. BECOMING MERE PAWNS

In a developing Asian country, there emerged a power-hungry politician with an insatiable appetite for wealth and influence. Cunning and ambitious, he was willing to bend morals and rewrite narratives to serve his own interests.

At the same time, a powerful business conglomerate had its eyes set on a prime stretch of land strategically located near a bustling port. The land promised immense commercial value, but there was one obstacle: it was inhabited by a marginalized minority community that had lived there for generations.

Seeing an opportunity, the politician struck a covert deal with the business house. What followed was a dark chapter orchestrated through manipulation and force. He unleashed loyal enforcers to stir unrest, fabricated stories about the minority population, and painted them as threats to national unity and security. With calculated rhetoric, he fanned the flames of division, exploiting existing prejudices and convincing the majority population that the land rightfully belonged to them.

Whipped into a frenzy by propaganda and lies, the majority community—unwitting pawns in a much larger scheme—rose against the minority residents. Violence erupted, homes were razed, and families were displaced. The land was cleared, not through legal means, but through fear and force.

In the aftermath, the government—under the influence of the politician—quietly transferred ownership of the now-vacant land to the business conglomerate for a fraction of its real value. The minority community was left shattered and homeless, the majority misled and used, while the politician and the business elite reaped their rewards in wealth and power.

Sometimes, without realizing it, we become mere pawns in someone else's carefully crafted scheme. Influenced by powerful figures or persuasive narratives, we may be led to believe we are fighting for justice or protecting our values, when in reality, we are being used to serve another's hidden agenda. These puppet masters, often driven by greed, power, or ambition, manipulate our emotions—anger, fear, pride—guiding our actions without our full awareness. In such moments, our sense of agency is quietly stripped away, and we act not from our own convictions, but from the will of those who see us as tools in their larger game.

In this state of manipulation, we may rise fiercely against those we are told are our enemies—our so-called opponents—only to discover too late that they were never the real threat. The people we confront, attack, or blame may be just as much victims as we are, caught in the same web of deceit. When the smoke clears and the truth begins to surface, we are left with the painful realization that our strength, our voice, and even our moral compass were hijacked. The real challenge then becomes reclaiming our awareness, questioning what we're told, and refusing to be used again—not by politicians, not by corporations, not by any force that thrives on division and blind loyalty.

55. THE FENCE

Alec once had an old apple tree that stood proudly in his backyard, offering a generous harvest of sweet, crisp fruits every year. It was more than just a tree—it was a symbol of growth, patience, and the quiet joy of nurturing something with care. Season after season, the tree bloomed and bore fruit, becoming part of Alec's daily rhythm. But as with all living things, time took its toll. The tree began to wither, its branches grew bare, and eventually, it died. Though saddened, Alec chose not to dwell on the loss. Instead, he saw it as an opportunity for renewal. At the edge of his backyard lawn, near a spot touched by both sun and shade, he planted a young apple sapling—hope rooted once more in the soil.

The area, however, was often visited by deer, graceful but notorious nibblers of tender leaves and shoots. Knowing the young sapling's vulnerability, Alec surrounded it with a simple, inexpensive plastic fence. It wasn't beautiful, but it served its purpose, acting as a barrier between the delicate new growth and the hungry intruders. Time passed, and the sapling stretched upward, its trunk thickening and branches spreading confidently toward the sky. When it had grown tall enough that the deer could no longer reach its foliage, Alec removed the protective fence. The tree now stood on its own, sturdy and resilient—no longer in need of shielding. It was a quiet triumph, a reminder that with care and patience, new life can flourish, even after loss.

When you are a parent, one of your greatest responsibilities is to protect your children—not only from physical harm but also from the many uncertainties and challenges the world presents. From their earliest days, children rely on their parents for comfort, guidance, and a sense of security. Parents strive to create a nurturing environment where their children can grow, explore, and develop their identity with confidence. They provide not just food and shelter, but wisdom gained through years of experience, helping their children navigate the complexities of life. This protection is a form of love, expressed through sleepless nights, careful decisions, and endless sacrifices.

However, this protection cannot—and should not—last forever. As children grow older, it becomes their duty to transform that foundation into their own strength. They must learn to take responsibility, to work diligently, and to carve out a path of their own. Life demands resilience, discipline, and a willingness to face hardship head-on. Parents cannot walk every step of the journey for them. Eventually, children must stand on their own, using the values and lessons passed down to them as tools to build their future. True success lies not in how long one leans on others, but in how confidently one can move forward without them.

A similar dynamic exists in the workplace between a senior officer and a junior employee. Just as a parent nurtures a child, a senior officer can provide initial guidance, mentorship, and support to help a younger or less experienced colleague grow. They may offer strategies, correct mistakes, and open doors to new opportunities. However, their role is not to handhold indefinitely. The mentorship they provide is meant to prepare the junior employee to take initiative, show leadership, and eventually rise in their own right. It is temporary scaffolding meant to support growth—not a permanent crutch.

Thus, it is the junior employee's responsibility to absorb that guidance, work hard, and eventually contribute fresh ideas and perspectives. They must learn to solve problems independently, adapt to challenges, and innovate within their field. Just as children must eventually step out from behind their parents, junior employees must earn the trust and respect of their peers through merit and creativity. While mentors and leaders can light the path, it is up to each individual to walk it. Growth—whether in the family or the professional world—comes when one moves from being protected to becoming capable.

56. THE WAGES OF WAR

The kingdoms of Nuland and Wesland had long been embroiled in a bitter conflict over a disputed stretch of land that both considered rightfully theirs. While Wesland was a vast and powerful realm with a well-equipped military and abundant resources, Nuland was a much smaller kingdom, both in size and strength. Despite their disadvantage, the rulers of Nuland were fiercely protective of their claim, and tensions between the two nations often flared into skirmishes along the border.

One particular incident escalated the conflict dramatically. Hoping to assert its authority and regain control of the contested region, Nuland launched a bold and aggressive military campaign. However, their forces were ill-prepared for the might of Wesland's army. The resulting battle was devastating: Wesland crushed Nuland's troops with brutal efficiency, leaving the smaller kingdom humiliated and weakened. The defeat sent shockwaves through Nuland, not just on the battlefield but also within its political leadership.

Disillusioned by the king's reckless decision to engage in a hopeless war, the governors of Nuland rose in rebellion. They viewed the king's actions as a betrayal of the people's trust and a danger to the kingdom's survival. Fueled by outrage and a desire for autonomy, the governors staged a coordinated revolt that quickly gained momentum. The king was overthrown, and with no central power to unite the land, Nuland fractured into four separate and independent kingdoms. Each new realm charted its own path, no longer bound by the ambitions of a single ruler, but the scars of war and division remained deeply etched into their shared history.

War is inherently risky, particularly for the leadership of a nation. Whether a country is ruled by a monarch or governed by a democratically elected official, the consequences of failure in warfare are often severe. A major military defeat can rapidly erode public confidence and political legitimacy. Leaders who lead their nations into unsuccessful conflicts frequently face immense pressure to step down, as both citizens and political rivals demand accountability for the loss and its aftermath.

In many cases, states that suffer defeat attempt to maintain unity through the use of propaganda or by crafting false narratives. These narratives often aim to shift blame, reinterpret the outcome, or glorify the sacrifice to preserve a sense of national purpose. By doing so, governments hope to prevent internal unrest and hold the country together despite the setback. However, these efforts may only be temporarily effective and can unravel quickly if other underlying issues are not addressed.

When a defeated nation is already facing economic hardship and lacks a strong cultural or ethnic cohesion among its population, the risks of fragmentation increase significantly. In such conditions, regional leaders or disillusioned groups may no longer see the benefit of remaining within a unified but failing state. Economic instability fuels discontent, while cultural differences make it harder to rally around a common identity. These factors can combine to push the nation toward division, as regions or factions seek independence or autonomy to pursue their own future apart from the failed central authority.

57. THE POWER OF INNOVATION

Every electronic device we see today—whether it's a smartphone, laptop, projector, or audio system—was once a bulky, heavy, and often expensive piece of machinery. In the early days of computing, for example, computers occupied entire rooms and required extensive infrastructure just to function. Similarly, early audio systems were large and cumbersome, often occupying significant space in homes or studios. Over time, advancements in technology have made it possible to reduce the size of these devices significantly while simultaneously increasing their efficiency, power, and affordability.

The miniaturization of electronics is a testament to the relentless pursuit of innovation. As new materials, components, and manufacturing techniques were developed, engineers and inventors found ways to reimagine what was possible. Circuit boards became smaller, batteries became more efficient, and wireless technologies eliminated the need for complex wiring. Each breakthrough opened the door to sleeker, more portable, and user-friendly designs. These changes didn't happen overnight—they evolved through consistent research, experimentation, and a willingness to challenge conventional limitations.

If you have an idea for a new electronic device—even if it seems bulky, impractical, or too expensive at first—do not be discouraged. Many of today's sleek gadgets began as prototypes that were large and costly. What matters most is the core function and the value it can provide. Once your idea is brought to market, feedback, competition, and ongoing innovation will naturally drive improvements. Costs will come down, designs will be refined, and your invention may eventually become a household staple.

This is the power of innovation: it transforms the impossible into the everyday. It reminds us that progress doesn't require perfection at the start—it requires vision, persistence, and the courage to begin. By embracing early challenges and imperfections, inventors pave the way for future breakthroughs. So whatever your idea may be, take that first step. The journey from bulky to brilliant begins with imagination and is propelled by innovation.

58. WHEELS OF CHANGE: TRACING INNOVATION FROM A HUMBLE BICYCLE

The bicycle, often seen as the simplest and cheapest mode of transport, holds a far more important place in human history than it appears at first glance. With two wheels, a frame, and a pair of pedals, the humble bicycle made independent travel accessible to the common person. It gave people the power to move faster and farther without relying on animals or public transport. But beyond its affordability and convenience, the bicycle sparked ideas that would eventually revolutionize modern transportation.

In the late 19th and early 20th centuries, inventors began experimenting with ways to add engines to bicycles. This led to the creation of the first motorized tricycles and quadricycles, the direct ancestors of the modern car. These early vehicles were essentially bicycles with engines—lightweight, open-framed, and steered by handlebars. The technology and mechanical knowledge used in building bicycles laid the foundation for many early automotive innovations, including steering systems, suspension, and rubber tires.

Even in the skies, the influence of the bicycle can be seen. The Wright brothers, credited with inventing the first powered airplane, were originally bicycle mechanics. Their deep understanding of balance, gear systems, and lightweight materials—skills developed from repairing and building bicycles—played a crucial role in their ability to create and fly the world's first airplane. Their journey from bicycles to airplanes is a powerful reminder of how even the simplest machines can inspire the most groundbreaking inventions.

At the heart of these innovations is something even more powerful than mechanics: human dreams. Every person carries a vision of what they want to achieve, something that pushes them forward. Dreams are what turn simple tools into world-changing ideas. Yet, most dreams face the same challenge—lack of money or resources. The Wright brothers, and many others like them, didn't wait for perfect conditions. Instead, they focused on accomplishing small goals, step by step, often using whatever they had.

In life, it's these small victories that build toward larger success. Every milestone you reach, no matter how minor it seems, brings you closer to fulfilling your dream. Whether you're riding a bicycle, building a machine, or chasing an idea, it all starts with determination and a willingness to keep going. The bicycle may be humble, but its story reminds us that great things often begin with simple steps— and that those steps, guided by dreams, can change the world.

59. THE THIRD ENTITY

In many families and communities, love, respect, and shared experiences are often believed to be the core elements of relationships. However, there exists a quiet, powerful force that shapes these bonds— money. It acts as a third entity, invisible but deeply influential. While we may think relationships are built solely on emotional connection, money often enters the picture and begins to define how we view and treat one another. It determines who speaks first, who is listened to, and who is quietly dismissed.

Within families, this influence can be especially sharp. Siblings raised under the same roof may grow apart not because of personal conflict, but because one becomes more financially successful. Conversations become strained, favors expected, and decisions swayed by who contributes the most financially. The elder without wealth may be ignored, while the younger with money gains authority. Respect becomes conditional, and love feels transactional. Even during family gatherings, money subtly dictates the seating arrangements, the tone of conversations, and who receives praise.

In society at large, the effect is even more pronounced. Friendships bend, alliances form, and reputations are built or broken based on income, possessions, or professional status. People often judge others not by their values or kindness, but by their wealth and influence. In this way, money silently mediates relationships, altering the way we connect and perceive each other. It becomes the third presence in every interaction, not seen but always felt—capable of strengthening or eroding even the most cherished human bonds.

60. UNTOUCHED FISH AND THE TAINTED FRIEND

A fish lives its entire life submerged in the ocean, surrounded by saltwater from the moment it is born until it dies. Yet, when we catch that fish and prepare it for a meal, we find that it doesn't taste salty. We must still season it, adding salt to bring out its flavor. This irony—that something so immersed in salt doesn't absorb its taste—serves as a metaphor for the nature of influence and change. Proximity doesn't always mean transformation.

This idea parallels human relationships, particularly long-standing friendships. You may grow up, study, and struggle side-by-side with someone through your school years. You share laughter, dreams, and hardships, believing your bond is unbreakable. In those formative years, status and wealth are rarely dividing lines. Your companionship feels immune to external pressures—much like the fish, untouched by the surrounding sea.

However, as life progresses and ambitions unfold, things can begin to shift. Your friend might rise in wealth, status, or power. With success often comes a change in priorities, perspectives, and even personality. Where once you were equals, now a gap emerges—a silent distance created not by geography but by life's hierarchy. The person you once knew may begin to act differently, subtly or overtly, and this change is most noticeable when you remain below their newfound status.

Unlike the fish, humans are susceptible to the environment of power and money. These forces, while external, can seep into a person's sense of identity and relationships. Suddenly, the friend who once stood by you may begin to speak differently, choose different circles, or even dismiss your presence. Their attitude becomes seasoned—not by time alone, but by the allure of what they have gained. It's not that success inherently corrupts, but that it reveals how deeply a person can be changed by it.

This transformation serves as a sobering reminder: long-standing familiarity doesn't guarantee consistency in character. Just as the fish resists the flavor of the sea, we hope that people can resist the distortions of wealth and status. But unlike fish, we are often influenced by our surroundings, and true character is tested not during shared struggle, but in the aftermath of success. The lesson is not only about the change in others, but also in how we respond—with grace, wisdom, and an unchanging sense of self.

61. FROM HOPE TO CONCERN

Claude, Clement and Claire had grown weary of their monotonous routines and longed for a break from the daily grind. Seeking peace and a change of scenery, they decided to leave the city behind and head into the woods as early summer set in. The idea of nature and solitude was refreshing, and they enjoyed walking among the trees and fresh air.

However, shortly after starting their journey back to the city, they noticed a couple of ticks crawling on the car seat. Aware of the health risks ticks pose, they pulled over immediately to inspect the vehicle and themselves thoroughly. They searched the car's interior and checked their clothing, eventually finding and carefully removing several ticks to prevent any possible spread of disease.

When children gain admission to a distant college, it often marks a major milestone not just in their lives, but also in the lives of their parents. Many families see this moment as the beginning of a journey filled with intellectual growth, personal development, and expanded opportunities. Parents send their children off with pride and hope, trusting that they will return home enriched by new experiences, wiser from their studies, and more prepared for the future.

However, the transition to college life can be challenging and unpredictable. Away from the familiar structure and guidance of home, some students struggle to adapt to their newfound independence. Peer pressure, academic stress, and the desire to fit in can lead them to adopt habits and behaviors that are harmful. These may include excessive partying, substance abuse, neglecting their studies, or developing unhealthy sleep and eating patterns.

When these students return home during holidays or breaks, their families sometimes find them changed—not in the positive ways they had imagined, but in ways that raise concern. Instead of bringing back maturity and insight, some return with attitudes or behaviors that strain relationships and pose risks to their physical and mental well-being. This disconnect can be painful for parents who had envisioned college as a stepping stone toward growth, only to find that their child may be drifting away from the values and discipline that once guided them.

62. VISIBLE AND INVISIBLE MILESTONES

As a student, each class represents a clear and tangible milestone in your educational journey, marking your progress in a structured and measurable way. With each academic year, you are presented with new subjects, challenges, and opportunities to grow both intellectually and personally. Successfully passing your exams at the end of the year is not only a validation of the knowledge and skills you've acquired but also a rite of passage that allows you to advance to the next level of learning. This progression from one grade to the next that is set by the education system gives students a sense of achievement and forward momentum, reinforcing the idea that dedication and hard work lead to measurable success. Each step forward builds upon the last, creating a continuous path of development that shapes your academic identity and prepares you for the future.

However, once you graduate from college or university and transition into the workforce, the clear and visible milestones that once guided your academic progress begin to fade. There are no more report cards, standardized tests, or official grade promotions to mark your development. Unlike school, where your advancement is mapped out and predictable, the professional world is far more fluid and undefined. You no longer move up just because a year has passed—you must now chart your own path and define success for yourself. This shift can feel disorienting at first, as the structure you once relied on is replaced with greater personal responsibility and self-direction.

In the workplace, milestones become largely invisible and must be intentionally set. These can take many forms: mastering a new skill, leading a project, earning a promotion, building a network, or achieving a specific goal you've identified. Unlike in school, where success is externally measured and universally understood, professional growth is often internal and subjective. You may not receive immediate recognition or feedback for your efforts, which makes it essential to establish clear personal and professional objectives. By doing so, you give yourself a sense of direction and purpose, enabling you to measure progress even when external validation is absent.

The milestones you set ultimately determine the trajectory of your career. They help you stay focused, motivated, and proactive in your development. Whether you aspire to become a leader in your field, transition to a different industry, or deepen your expertise in a specialized area, the goals you create and the effort you invest in achieving them shape your professional identity. In this way, success after school is less about moving through a predesigned system and more about building your own ladder—one rung at a time.

63. BEFORE YOU GO: ONE LAST LOOK

Josh was the head of the marketing division at a major corporation, a role that placed him at the heart of high-stakes deals and strategic planning. After months of rigorous negotiation, long conference calls, and meticulous revisions, he finally closed a landmark agreement with a prestigious new client—one of the largest contracts in the company's history. The deal represented a turning point not just for his team, but for the company as a whole.

To finalize the agreement, Josh flew to a bustling metropolitan city, home to the client's global headquarters. After a formal meeting filled with handshakes, signatures, and quiet celebration, the contract was officially signed. With the job seemingly complete, he returned to his hotel, exhausted but satisfied. That night, he reviewed the signed documents carefully, double-checked every detail, and placed the folder on the corner table beside the window—safe, but temporarily out of sight.

The next morning was a blur. Josh spent hours fielding calls from colleagues and clients, updating them on the successful deal and coordinating next steps. Amid the flurry of conversations, the hotel front desk rang to inform him that his taxi to the airport had arrived. Realizing he was short on time, Josh scrambled to pack his belongings, tossing clothes and chargers into his suitcase in a hurry.

As he slung his bag over his shoulder and reached for the door, a nagging feeling stopped him. He paused and glanced back across the room. There, barely visible in the corner where the sunlight was just beginning to stream in, was the signed contract—the critical document that had taken months to secure. His heart skipped a beat.

Had he left it behind, the consequences could have been catastrophic. Not only would the company have been exposed to significant legal and financial risk, but the breach of trust with the client could have undone everything he had worked so hard to build. In the wrong hands, that document could have spelled disaster.

With a deep breath, Josh retrieved the folder, tucked it safely into his briefcase, and left the room with a renewed sense of caution—and a quiet reminder that even in victory, vigilance is everything.

It's always important to take a final look around your room before leaving a hotel or guest house. This last check can help ensure you haven't left behind any personal belongings such as chargers, toiletries, clothing, or important documents. Items can easily slip behind furniture, get mixed up in bedsheets, or be left in drawers and closets. Taking just a few extra minutes to scan the room thoroughly can save you the stress and inconvenience of losing something valuable or having to arrange for it to be shipped back to you later.

Beyond checking for forgotten items, doing a final walkthrough of your hotel or guest house room allows you to make sure everything is left in proper order. Take a moment to turn off the lights, unplug any electronics, and ensure that all windows and doors are securely closed or locked. These small actions not only contribute to energy conservation and safety but also demonstrate respect for the property and those who maintain it.

Taking a few extra steps—such as tidying up the room, making the bed, or leaving a tip with a note of gratitude for the housekeeping staff—further reflects courtesy and appreciation. These thoughtful gestures acknowledge the efforts of those who help make your stay comfortable and leave a positive impression behind. Ultimately, a careful final check is a simple but meaningful habit that highlights your sense of responsibility, both to your own belongings and to the space you've used.

64. ELITE SCHOOL EDUCATION

Students typically enroll in colleges and universities with the goal of acquiring knowledge, learning new skills, and building networks that can support their future careers. Through a structured curriculum, they study a wide range of subjects related to their field of interest and participate in hands-on projects, discussions, and assessments. Most conventional educational systems also include opportunities for students to engage in internships, where they gain practical experience by working in real-world environments. These internships often serve as stepping stones, allowing students to develop professional connections and demonstrate their capabilities to potential employers. However, even with a degree and internship experience, many students still face the challenge of attending dozens of job interviews before securing a position.

The traditional path to employment is not always straightforward. In many cases, students must refine their resumes, practice interview techniques, and tailor applications to each job they pursue. Despite their academic achievements, they find themselves competing in a crowded job market where qualifications alone may not guarantee employment. The process can be lengthy and uncertain, requiring persistence, patience, and resilience.

Networking events, job fairs, and mentorship programs become crucial tools to navigate this phase, helping students stand out in a sea of applicants.

In contrast, elite universities offer a dramatically different experience. These institutions often have access to cutting-edge resources, world-class faculty, and deep industry connections. Students at such universities are not merely learning from textbooks—they are immersed in the latest research, working with emerging technologies, and tackling complex, real-world problems. The focus shifts from rote memorization to innovation and critical thinking. Courses may be designed in collaboration with industry leaders, ensuring that students are trained in the most current methodologies and tools relevant to their field.

Furthermore, students at elite institutions are frequently encouraged to pursue their own ideas and entrepreneurial ventures. Instead of waiting to join an existing company, they are empowered to create one. They collaborate with peers across disciplines to develop solutions to pressing global issues, often securing patents and research grants while still in school. These projects can evolve into startups and businesses, supported by university incubators, venture capital networks, and mentorship from successful alumni. The ecosystem fosters a culture of innovation where students are not just preparing for the future—they are actively shaping it.

By the time students from elite universities graduate, many are already running their own companies or leading major research initiatives. They transition from academia to entrepreneurship with a head start, bypassing the traditional job-seeking process altogether. Their education has not only equipped them with technical skills but also the confidence, vision, and leadership needed to drive change. While both traditional and elite educational paths have value, the latter clearly opens doors to greater autonomy, influence, and impact from a much earlier stage in one's career.

65. PARENTAL SUPPORT INSPIRES STUDENT SUCCESS

Austin planted an apple tree in his backyard with great excitement, envisioning the day it would bear crisp, delicious fruit. But just a few days later, his hopes were dashed when he discovered that deer had found the young tree and chewed up its tender branches and leaves. The damage was severe, and the sapling could not be saved. Though disappointed, Austin did not allow the setback to discourage him. Instead, he resolved to try again, this time with better preparation and greater determination.

He returned to the nursery and purchased another apple tree. Determined to protect it, Austin built a sturdy fence around the new sapling to keep deer away. He cleared the surrounding area of weeds so the tree wouldn't have to compete for nutrients, and he made sure to water it consistently during the hot summer months. He also enriched the soil with fertilizer to encourage healthy growth. His efforts were rewarded a couple of years later when the tree bloomed with flowers, eventually producing plump, juicy apples.

In today's world, parents are generally more educated and technologically proficient than those of previous generations. With greater access to information, modern parents are better equipped to support their children's academic journeys. Schools now assign creative and research-based projects starting from early grades, requiring children not only to understand academic content but also to apply it in meaningful ways. These projects often involve digital tools, research skills, and creative presentation formats—areas where tech-savvy parents can provide valuable guidance.

When children are assigned school projects, parents face a choice: they can either ignore the assignments and leave their children to figure things out on their own, or they can take an active role by working alongside them. While fostering independence is important, children often lack the experience or skills needed to navigate complex tasks entirely by themselves. When parents show interest and participate in the process—offering guidance, helping with research, or brainstorming creative ideas—children feel supported and encouraged. This collaboration can turn what might have been a stressful task into an enjoyable learning experience.

Moreover, when parents engage in school projects with their children, it sends a powerful message: that learning is valuable and worth the time and effort of both child and adult. This involvement boosts the child's motivation, deepens their understanding, and strengthens the parent-child bond. Children become more confident in their abilities and are more likely to approach future assignments with enthusiasm. In this way, parental involvement doesn't just improve project outcomes—it also nurtures a lifelong love of learning.

66. BEYOND CAPITAL: THE TRUE DRIVERS OF CORPORATE SUCCESS

Tyson was a highly accomplished businessman and visionary leader. Through relentless hard work, strategic decision-making, and a deep understanding of the market, he built his company into a powerhouse that delivered strong revenues year after year. His leadership style was admired across the corporate world, and his company eventually became a benchmark for success, earning a coveted spot in the Dow Jones Industrial Average. Tyson's influence extended beyond the business world—he represented the nation at international economic forums and served as a trusted advisor to the President on matters of commerce and innovation.

Despite his achievements, Tyson's early life was marked by hardship and responsibility. He lost his father at a young age, a devastating blow that forced him to grow up quickly. As the eldest child, Tyson took on the role of caretaker for his younger siblings, supporting his mother as she held the family together. She instilled in him the values of discipline, resilience, and the importance of living a life rooted in simplicity and integrity. These lessons became the foundation for Tyson's character and the driving force behind his later success.

Tyson and his mother managed their modest household with grace and determination. While pursuing his education, Tyson worked part-time jobs to contribute to the family's finances. He remained committed to his siblings' futures, helping them secure scholarships and educational opportunities at top-tier universities. Through careful planning, hard work, and a deep sense of duty, Tyson ensured that each of them received a high-quality education. Eventually all of them became leaders in their domain.

A company's success and wealth are not determined solely by its financial resources. While capital is undoubtedly important for operations and expansion, it is not the only driving force behind a thriving enterprise. Many businesses with vast financial backing have failed due to poor leadership, lack of innovation, or inefficient management. In contrast, some companies with modest funding have risen to great heights because of visionary leadership, strategic planning, and a strong internal culture. Financial assets are merely one part of a larger equation that determines long-term sustainability.

What truly sets successful companies apart is their passion for continuous improvement and innovation. Organizations that prioritize developing new products, refining services, and responding creatively to market needs are often the ones that lead their industries. These companies are not afraid to take risks, challenge the status quo, and invest in research and development. Their forward-thinking approach keeps them ahead of competitors and earns customer loyalty. Innovation becomes part of the company's DNA, fueling both growth and relevance in a fast-changing world.

Equally important is the ability to manage internal costs efficiently. Companies that carefully control their operating expenses without compromising on quality often find themselves in stronger positions during economic downturns. Streamlining processes, reducing waste, and maintaining lean operations can lead to higher profit margins and greater flexibility. Financial health is not just about how much a company earns—it's also about how wisely it spends. When financial prudence is combined with innovation and purpose, a company is well-positioned for sustainable success.

67. TAKING THE FIRST STEP TO LEARN

Any dedicated educator will affirm that teaching becomes truly effective when a student takes the first step toward learning. That initial step—showing interest, asking questions, or simply being open to instruction—signals a readiness to grow. Without that willingness, even the most skilled teacher will struggle to make progress. Students who remain disengaged or indifferent, metaphorically "in the ditch," are difficult to reach because they lack the internal drive necessary for learning to take root.

For learning to thrive, students must be willing to work hard and actively seek out new knowledge. Taking initiative, whether by practicing outside of class, exploring topics independently, or asking for help, demonstrates a hunger to improve. These are the students who are easiest to teach—not because they are naturally gifted, but because their attitude and effort create a strong foundation. Their motivation acts as a bridge between the educator's guidance and their own progress.

Ambition also plays a vital role in a student's success. When students have a clear goal or dream they are working toward, they become more focused, resilient, and driven. Educators can then tailor instruction to help students connect their learning to real-life aspirations.

Over time, these motivated learners absorb new skills and concepts more easily, setting themselves on a path toward personal and academic achievement. In essence, the combination of effort, initiative, and ambition creates a student who is not only teachable but destined to succeed.

Like young students, adults benefit from mentorship only when they are open and willing to learn. Growth at any stage requires humility and a desire to improve. Those who see learning as a lifelong journey welcome new ideas, while rigid and fossilized minds bound by past experiences or outdated knowledge struggle to adapt in a changing world.

An essential part of being teachable is self-awareness—understanding one's own limitations and being honest about areas that need improvement. Ego, however, often stands as a major barrier to this process. When individuals let pride cloud their judgment, they may feel threatened by correction or feedback, viewing it as a challenge rather than an opportunity. True learning requires setting aside ego and embracing vulnerability. Only then can mentors effectively guide and support personal or professional development, leading to meaningful transformation.

68. DELAYED BUT DESTINED

Bernard hurried through the bustling streets of the city, his mind racing with the details of the critical client meeting scheduled for 9:00 AM sharp. The morning had not gone according to plan—he had been delayed at home due to unexpected family matters, and his drive to the office was worsened by unusually heavy traffic. Glancing at the dashboard clock with growing anxiety, he knew he was cutting it dangerously close. By the time he arrived at the towering company headquarters, his heart was pounding with both stress and urgency as he sprinted into the lobby and made a beeline for the elevators.

To his dismay, a small crowd had already gathered in front of one elevator that had just opened its doors. The space inside was already packed with employees and visitors, and Bernard's eyes quickly scanned the group to spot his clients standing among the passengers. He tried to squeeze in, but there was no room left. The elevator doors slid shut with a soft ding, and Bernard was left standing outside, a sinking feeling settling in his chest. He felt defeated, certain that this missed elevator meant he would be late to a meeting that could shape the future of his career. He stood alone in front of the other elevators, watching the lobby floor anxiously as he waited for another chance.

Just then, one of the other elevators descended and opened its doors, revealing an empty interior. Without hesitation, Bernard stepped inside, grateful for the unexpected opportunity. The elevator began its ascent, and since he was the sole occupant, it made no stops along the way. To his surprise and relief, he arrived at the thirtieth floor well before the crowded elevator reached it. As he stepped out into the hallway, he allowed himself a deep breath and a small smile. Despite the chaotic start to his morning, he had arrived on time, and now had a few precious moments to collect himself before the important meeting began.

There are times in life when it feels as though your efforts go unnoticed, especially when you see others around you being promoted or rewarded while you continue to toil without recognition. You work diligently, put in long hours, and strive to meet every expectation, yet others—sometimes seemingly with less effort—advance ahead of you. This disparity can lead to deep frustration and self-doubt. You begin to question why life feels unfair, why fate seems to favor others while you're left behind, despite giving your best in every task.

However, what often goes unseen during these periods of delay is the foundation being quietly laid for something greater. While others may experience quicker but smaller successes, your slower journey may be allowing you to develop a broader skill set, gain deeper experience, and build resilience. These periods of waiting and working in the shadows can shape you in profound ways—refining your character, sharpening your abilities, and preparing you for responsibilities that go beyond the scope of a routine promotion. You might be mastering skills across multiple areas, cultivating a versatility that many of your peers may lack.

In the long run, this path of steady growth can place you in a position far more influential and impactful than the ones others rushed into. While they may celebrate early victories, your delayed progress could ultimately catapult you further up the ladder, equipping you not just for a higher title, but for a role of greater significance and purpose. Life's apparent setbacks can, in hindsight, be setups for breakthroughs that exceed your original expectations. Patience, perseverance, and continuous self-improvement may quietly be leading you to a destiny that rewards not just your work, but your wisdom and readiness as well.

69. HISTORY MOLDS THE PERSONALITY

People vary widely in how they experience and engage in social interaction. Some individuals naturally enjoy being in the presence of others, finding stimulation and joy in conversation, laughter, and shared experiences. These people often feel alive and connected when they are surrounded by friends, family, or even strangers. Social environments fuel their energy and provide a sense of belonging. For them, human connection is not just enjoyable—it's essential to their well-being.

On the other hand, many people prefer solitude over constant interaction. For these more introverted individuals, time spent alone is not a sign of sadness or isolation but a necessary retreat to recharge and reflect. They often find fulfillment in solitary activities such as reading, writing, listening to music, or exploring nature. Quiet moments allow them to process their thoughts deeply, free from the demands and expectations that can come with social settings. In this sense, loneliness becomes a space for personal growth rather than something to be avoided.

The differences in social behavior are not purely based on personality but are often shaped by personal history. People who have experienced emotional pain, such as abandonment, betrayal, or abuse, may develop a strong preference for being alone. Their withdrawal can be a form of self-protection, a way to avoid the risk of further emotional harm. In many cases, these individuals are not antisocial; rather, they have learned to be cautious due to past wounds that have not fully healed.

Moreover, communication experiences also play a significant role in shaping one's willingness to engage socially. Those whose words have been misunderstood, mocked, or shared inappropriately may lose confidence in speaking up. This can lead to a reluctance to participate in conversations, even when they have much to say. Over time, this pattern can become ingrained, making people appear distant or uncommunicative when, in reality, they are simply protecting themselves from emotional discomfort or judgment.

Ultimately, the way people relate to others is deeply personal and influenced by both their innate disposition and their life experiences. Some thrive in vibrant social circles, while others find peace in solitude. Some are naturally expressive, while others learn to guard their voice. Recognizing and respecting these differences is essential to understanding human behavior and fostering compassion. Everyone carries a unique story that shapes how they connect—or choose not to connect— with the world around them.

70. ENDURANCE IN EXILE

Norman was assigned to a remote rural village, far removed from the comfort and conveniences of the bustling city. He had been selected to oversee and implement a critical energy project intended to improve infrastructure in the area. The nature of his work required him to stay in the village for a minimum of two months. Though he had undertaken challenging assignments before, this was unlike anything he had experienced. The distance, isolation, and unfamiliar environment posed both professional and personal challenges.

The village itself was impoverished and underdeveloped. Basic amenities were scarce, and living conditions were harsh. The only accommodation available was a dilapidated hotel that had clearly seen better days. With crumbling walls, leaky roofs, and limited utilities, it offered little comfort. Still, Norman made it his temporary home, returning there each night after long days spent in the field conducting surveys, supervising installations, and meeting with local stakeholders. It wasn't ideal, but it served its purpose.

Despite the discomfort and fatigue, Norman maintained his focus. His mission was clear: bring energy access to a community that had lived in darkness for too long. Over the weeks, he grew accustomed to the rhythms of village life and even found a sense of purpose in the work he was doing. The gratitude and hope he saw in the eyes of the villagers became his motivation. When the project was finally completed, Norman returned to his office in the city—tired, but fulfilled, knowing he had helped lay the groundwork for progress.

Reflecting on his experience, Norman realized how unpredictable life could be. Sometimes, due to unforeseen circumstances, we may lose everything we once held dear—even the homes we built with care. In such moments, we might find ourselves in unfamiliar and less fortunate places, forced to adapt to harsh realities. Yet, it is in these very moments of hardship that we must resist the urge to dwell on what was and instead look forward to what could be.

Life's difficult seasons are not permanent. They test our character and resilience but do not define our future. Norman's time in the village served as a reminder that tough times do not last—but tough people do. By enduring challenges and choosing to persevere, we can rebuild, rise, and work toward a brighter future, no matter how dark the present may seem.

71. VALUE OF HUMAN POTENTIAL

Postage stamps undergo meticulous sorting and quality control processes before they are released into circulation. This scrutiny ensures that only flawless stamps are distributed for public use, maintaining the integrity and standard of postal services. Each stamp is carefully examined for printing accuracy, correct denomination, proper alignment, and overall appearance. Despite these strict inspections, on rare occasions, stamps with printing flaws or production anomalies manage to slip through and enter circulation. These mistakes, although unintended, are of great interest to collectors and philatelists due to their rarity and uniqueness.

When a postage stamp with an error reaches the public, it often becomes highly sought-after and can fetch a significant price at auctions. Common types of errors include inverted or misaligned images, incorrect denomination or pricing, mistakes in the printed legend or text, color inconsistencies, ink smudges, errors in overprinting, and missing or irregular perforations. These flaws transform otherwise ordinary stamps into valuable collector's items. The more unusual and well-documented the error, the greater the interest from collectors, sometimes elevating the stamp's value to many times its original worth.

By default, every human being is born with a similar capacity for growth, learning, and expression. While we all share the basic potential to think, feel, and create, our individual experiences, interests, and opportunities shape the specific talents we develop over time. Human beings possess a wide range of abilities, and the foundation for greatness lies within everyone. However, not everyone nurtures or discovers their full potential in the same way.

Among the vast sea of human potential, certain individuals rise to prominence because of their exceptional gifts in areas like music, art, literature, business, or innovation. These individuals often dedicate years to mastering their craft, pushing boundaries, and offering new perspectives that resonate with others. Society naturally takes notice of such talent, celebrating it not just for its uniqueness but also for its ability to enrich culture, inspire emotions, and spark progress.

As a result, people who excel in these domains frequently receive widespread recognition and admiration. Their contributions often lead to financial rewards, including royalties from their creative works, inventions, or business ventures. These royalties not only reflect the value society places on their talents but also serve as a lasting form of compensation for the impact they've made. While everyone starts with the same fundamental potential, those who cultivate their abilities in remarkable ways often find their work immortalized and rewarded.

72. MASTERING THE ART OF QUICK LEARNING IN THE DIGITAL AGE

When professional singers arrive at the music studio, they are guided through the creative process by the composer, who plays a central role in shaping their performance. The composer not only introduces the singers to the song but also teaches them its melody, rhythm, emotional tone, and intended interpretation, often sharing the inspiration behind the lyrics and guiding them through any challenging parts. These accomplished vocalists, with their refined skills and quick adaptability, study the piece closely, internalizing its nuances and rehearsing it thoroughly—often within just a few hours. Once they feel confident, they step into the recording booth to deliver a polished performance, typically recording multiple takes to capture the best possible version. After the recording session, the track goes through post-production, where it is mixed and mastered to achieve the highest sound quality. Finally, the finished song is released and distributed, reaching audiences around the globe, where it becomes part of the musical landscape for listeners everywhere to enjoy.

In today's digital age, information is more accessible than ever before. With just a few clicks or taps, we can access a vast array of knowledge on virtually any topic, thanks to the internet. Whether it's academic subjects, professional development, creative skills, or practical life hacks, there are countless videos, articles, tutorials, and online courses designed to teach and guide learners at every level. From cooking and coding to music theory and medical research, the resources available are as diverse as they are abundant. This ease of access has eliminated many traditional barriers to learning, allowing anyone with curiosity and determination to acquire new knowledge and skills without the need for formal classrooms or expensive institutions.

However, with this incredible opportunity comes a responsibility—one that falls on each individual. It is our duty to take initiative, harness the power of these resources, and commit ourselves to mastering the techniques that can help us grow personally and professionally. Simply having access to information is not enough; true progress comes through discipline, effort, and consistent application of what we learn. In a world that is constantly evolving, those who make lifelong learning a habit will be better equipped to adapt, innovate, and thrive. The tools are there—what matters now is how we choose to use them.

73. THE FRAGILE NATURE OF SUCCESS-BASED FRIENDSHIPS

Toby the hamster was eager to try out his brand-new hamster wheel, excited by the idea of a fun and healthy workout. At first, he found the spinning exhilarating—the wind rushing past his tiny ears and the rhythm of his little paws hitting the wheel filled him with joy. His friends gathered around, clapping their paws and shouting words of encouragement, proud of his enthusiasm and determination. But as the minutes passed and the wheel kept turning, Toby began to grow weary; his legs ached, his breath came in short gasps, and his excitement slowly faded into exhaustion. Unable to continue, he finally leapt off the wheel, panting heavily. Instead of offering sympathy or support, his friends burst into laughter, mocking his early exit and calling him a quitter, leaving Toby embarrassed and disheartened.

When you are wealthy and successful, your friends often become your loudest cheerleaders. They admire your achievements, celebrate your victories, and bask in the glow of your success. Your actions, no matter how small, are met with praise and enthusiasm, and your social circle seems full of support and admiration. The benefits of your status ripple outward, drawing people toward you with encouragement and warmth.

However, this admiration is often conditional. The moment you experience a significant failure or setback, the tone can change abruptly. Friends who once applauded your every move may begin to pull away. Instead of offering empathy or encouragement, some may criticize your decisions or question your abilities. Failure becomes a source of judgment rather than an opportunity for growth, and the very people who once lifted you up may now contribute to your sense of isolation.

In some cases, this shift reveals the superficial nature of certain relationships. Wealth and success can attract those more interested in what you represent than who you are. When the outer layers of achievement are stripped away, true character—yours and theirs—is exposed. Genuine friends will remain by your side through failure, but fair-weather companions often vanish, leaving behind a harsh lesson about the fragility of social bonds built on status rather than substance.

74. THE ART OF COMMUNICATION

It was a warm summer afternoon, and the park lay mostly quiet under the soft golden sunlight. The air was still, with only a gentle rustling of leaves breaking the calm. Few people were around—just a handful of families scattered under trees or walking along the paths. In one corner of the park, a group of children played happily, their laughter echoing lightly through the air as their parents watched over them from nearby benches or blankets spread across the grass.

Sam and his four-year-old son, Charlie, were strolling together when something on the ground caught Charlie's attention. He tugged at his father's hand and pointed, asking curiously, "What is that?" Sam bent down and picked up the object. "It's a pen," he replied. Charlie, unfamiliar with the word, tilted his head and asked, "What's a pen?" With a small smile, Sam explained, "A pen is a tool used for writing. It has a plastic tube filled with ink. People use it to write words and draw pictures." Charlie nodded thoughtfully, trying to understand, as he gazed at the seemingly ordinary object now holding a bit of mystery.

A little while later, Percy and his son Philip walked past the same spot. Philip, noticing the pen lying on the grass again, asked his father what it was. "It's a pen," Percy said, picking it up. Then, he added with a note of reflection, "A pen is an instrument for writing or drawing. But more than that, it's powerful. The pen is mightier than any weapon. Through it, we share our thoughts and ideas with the world." Philip looked up at his father, eyes wide with interest. "Can I have it?" he asked. "Of course," Percy replied, handing it to him. "It seems someone lost it." That small moment, perhaps forgotten by others, stayed with Philip—who, years later, would become a well-known author, his words shaping thoughts just as his father once said.

The way you communicate your message plays a crucial role in how it is received and understood. Whether you're speaking to one person or addressing a large audience, the tone, clarity, and structure of your message determine its impact. A well-delivered message can inspire, persuade, or educate, while a poorly communicated one can lead to confusion or indifference. Sometimes, even the most brilliant ideas fail to make an impression simply because they were not expressed effectively.

Communication also depends on the intent and depth of explanation. Any topic—no matter how complex—can either be brushed aside with a vague statement or explored in great detail with patience and care. For example, someone may dismiss a serious issue with a simple phrase like "it's nothing," while another person might choose to break it down thoughtfully, offering background, reasoning, and context. The difference lies in how much the speaker values clarity and how much the listener is willing to engage. In many cases, people respond not just to what you say, but how deeply and sincerely you say it.

Furthermore, the art of delivering a message includes knowing your audience. The same idea might be explained differently to a child, a friend, or a professional group. Tailoring your words to match the listener's understanding and interests shows thoughtfulness and improves the chances of your message being heard and remembered. Ultimately, communication is not just about transferring information—it's about building understanding. Whether you skim the surface or dive deep, how you present your thoughts will shape how they live on in others' minds.

75. THE UNSUNG SUPPORTERS BEHIND EVERY GRADUATE

Gregory made his way to the local bakery with a clear purpose in mind: to pick out the perfect birthday cake for his son. The display cases were filled with a vibrant array of cakes, each one standing out with its own distinct combination of icing colors and decorative touches. Some were adorned with bright sprinkles, others with intricate piping or sugar flowers. Despite their varied appearances, Gregory noticed that they all shared one common element—the inside was always the same moist, yellow vanilla cake. It was a classic flavor, simple yet comforting, and a favorite among both kids and adults.

After scanning the selection carefully, Gregory decided on a cake that struck the perfect balance of festive and elegant. He chose one frosted in smooth swirls of blue and white, the colors blending like clouds in a summer sky. To top it off, a single glossy cherry sat at the center, adding a pop of color and a playful finishing touch. It wasn't the most elaborate cake in the display, but something about its cheerful simplicity felt just right for his son's celebration. Satisfied with his choice, Gregory smiled, already imagining the look of delight on his son's face when the candles were lit.

When children begin their educational journey, the financial responsibility typically falls on their parents. In the early years, this includes tuition fees, school supplies, uniforms, and other miscellaneous expenses, which most families manage without significant hardship. As students advance through the education system, however, the cost of schooling increases substantially. Reaching the terminal degree—whether it be a university bachelor's, master's, or professional certification—often requires significantly higher tuition, specialized materials, and living expenses, particularly if the student must relocate or attend a private institution. At this stage, many parents may find themselves unable to bear the financial burden alone.

In such circumstances, the responsibility of funding a child's final stages of education may shift to other sources. Older siblings sometimes step in, working extra jobs or contributing a portion of their income to support their younger family members. Relatives—such as uncles, aunts, or grandparents—may also provide financial aid, recognizing the long-term value of a good education. Additionally, scholarships awarded by charitable foundations or educational institutions can offer a lifeline to deserving students based on merit or need. For those without access to these forms of assistance, student loans from banks become an alternative path, helping students bridge the gap between ambition and affordability. These loans, while useful, also carry the weight of future repayment, making the decision to borrow a serious and consequential one.

When graduates enter the workforce and begin applying for jobs, employers typically focus on the terminal degree listed on the resume. The name of the institution, the major, and the final qualification are often all that matter in determining a candidate's potential. Rarely do employers ask where the student's journey began, the obstacles they faced, or who supported them along the way. Yet, that degree—a gateway to opportunity—is often the result of many sacrifices made behind the scenes. Like a well-made cake, every part of the academic journey must be solid and meaningful. Icing can only be applied to a cake with a firm foundation; similarly, the value of a degree is built on years of perseverance and support.

The people who offer financial aid, emotional encouragement, or practical help during this final stage of education play a transformative role in a graduate's life. Their contributions often determine whether a student can cross the finish line or not. These supporters— parents, mentors, friends, or even strangers— enable students to chase dreams that might otherwise be unreachable. Their investment doesn't just help complete an academic milestone; it helps shape a future. While the diploma may bear only one name, the achievement belongs to many. Recognizing the invisible hands behind the success adds depth and gratitude to the celebration of any graduation.

76. HIDDEN INTENTIONS

When Shane began his studies at the university, he was placed in a three-member team for laboratory sessions. Each team in the class was given a dedicated cabinet to store their reagents and plastic wares. Shane's team included Sarah and Reese, and they shared responsibilities in the lab, working together to complete their assignments. The cabinets served as shared storage spaces and were essential for organizing their materials efficiently.

Shane regularly visited the library to collect textbooks and other study materials, which he generously shared with Sarah and Reese. He valued teamwork and ensured everyone had access to the necessary resources. Sarah, who came from a single-parent household, often received extra support from both Shane and Reese. They made a conscious effort to help her whenever possible, trying to ease any challenges she might face during their rigorous academic journey.

As the program neared its end, students were required to undertake an independent scientific project. For this, each student was assigned an individual cabinet to store their project materials. Interestingly, Sarah was assigned the same cabinet that had been used by their original team. This arrangement didn't seem unusual at first, and everyone focused on preparing for their projects.

One day, as Shane planned a trip to the city to collect some books, Sarah asked him to pick up a lock and key. Shane found the request slightly curious, but agreed without questioning her intentions.

Upon returning, Shane handed the lock and key to Sarah. To his surprise, she used them in an unexpected way. Sarah opened the cabinet they once shared, removed Shane's bottle of reagent, placed it on the lab bench, locked the cabinet with her new lock, and walked away without a word. It was a moment that revealed an entirely different side of her—one Shane hadn't seen before. Her quiet request had masked a hidden intention, and the trust that once defined their teamwork was suddenly fractured.

The mind is like a vast ocean—deep, mysterious, and ever-changing. Just as the surface may appear calm while powerful currents swirl beneath, the true intentions of the mind often remain hidden, unpredictable, and difficult to fully understand.

77. MARKETING MATTERS

Syd opened a quaint bakery in a small town, offering fresh and flavorful baked goods that quickly won the hearts of local residents. To gain a competitive edge over an established bakery in town, Syd enlisted the help of his nephew Johann, a budding advertising entrepreneur. Johann used traditional marketing tactics—flyers, word-of-mouth, and local newspaper ads—to promote the bakery. These efforts brought moderate success, with Syd's baked goods gaining popularity not only within the town but also in nearby communities. Still, Syd understood that Johann's methods lacked the sophistication and reach of modern marketing, limiting the potential for broader growth.

Years later, Syd's son Anderson joined the family business with a bold vision: to transform the small-town bakery into a nationally recognized brand. Aware of the evolving marketing landscape, Anderson partnered with a prominent marketing firm in the city known for its creative campaigns. The firm implemented cutting-edge strategies, including product placements in popular films, where Syd's bakery goods were featured in dining scenes. This subtle yet effective exposure introduced the brand to a national audience, elevating its profile and attracting widespread attention. Thanks to Anderson's forward-thinking approach and the firm's innovative outreach, the bakery began to evolve from a local favorite into a household name.

Advertisement and marketing are essential components in the success of fast-moving consumer goods (FMCGs). These products, which include everyday items like food, beverages, toiletries, and cleaning supplies, rely heavily on visibility, brand recall, and consumer trust. In a market saturated with choices, even high-quality products can go unnoticed without effective promotion. Businesses must continuously adapt to changing consumer behaviors, digital trends, and competitive strategies. Simply put, no matter how excellent the product is, without strong marketing, it will struggle to survive in today's fast-paced marketplace.

Innovation in marketing is no longer a luxury— it's a necessity. Companies must think beyond traditional advertisements and embrace modern, data-driven approaches such as social media campaigns, influencer partnerships, experiential marketing, and targeted digital advertising. Relying on outdated or unimaginative strategies can cause a brand to stagnate. Moreover, decisions based on personal relationships rather than professional merit can be detrimental. Just because someone is a family member or a close friend does not mean they have the expertise or tools needed to compete in a dynamic industry. In business, sentimentality should not override practicality.

Poor marketing doesn't just slow growth—it can derail an entire company. A weak campaign can lead to low sales, loss of consumer interest, and a damaged reputation, all of which are difficult to recover from. When consumers fail to connect with a brand or are unaware of its presence, even the best products will gather dust on shelves. To succeed, businesses must invest in competent, forward-thinking marketing professionals and agencies that understand market trends and consumer psychology. In the end, choosing the right marketing strategy is not just about selling products—it's about securing the future of the business.

78. LIVING IN THE FAST LANE

Highways are typically divided into three lanes, each serving a different purpose based on speed. The left lane, often called the "fast lane," is intended for vehicles traveling at higher speeds, typically above the legal limit, though still within safe and reasonable bounds. The middle lane is generally for those maintaining the posted speed limit—it's a balanced zone for steady, uninterrupted travel. Meanwhile, the right lane is usually reserved for slower-moving vehicles, merging traffic, or those exiting the highway. This structure helps regulate the flow of traffic, allowing vehicles to travel efficiently and safely based on their speed and driving needs.

Drivers often self-sort based on their confidence, vehicle performance, and driving conditions. Elderly drivers and large trucks tend to stick to the right lane, where slower speeds are safer and more manageable. In contrast, younger drivers or those with high-performance, modern vehicles often favor the left lane, aiming for swift, seamless travel. However, it's important for drivers in the left lane to maintain a consistent high speed—lingering or slowing down can frustrate faster drivers behind them and disrupt the flow. If a driver in the left lane begins to feel fatigued or uncomfortable maintaining a fast pace, it's courteous and safer to shift to the middle lane, allowing more energetic or capable drivers to pass. This lane discipline not only enhances safety but also ensures smoother traffic movement for everyone.

In the world of technology, staying ahead means being a pioneer. It's not enough to simply understand the current tools and trends—you must be among those shaping the future. Technology is a rapidly evolving field, where new discoveries, tools, and methods emerge almost daily. To remain relevant, professionals must lead the charge by exploring uncharted territory, solving complex problems, and creating solutions that others haven't yet imagined. Being a pioneer means embracing uncertainty, taking risks, and being unafraid to challenge the status quo.

Lifelong innovation is not optional; it's essential. The moment you become comfortable or stop seeking better ways to do things, the world begins to pass you by. Others, driven by fresh ideas and bold ambition, will rise and take your place. The tech landscape is littered with companies and individuals who once led the field but failed to adapt. Innovation isn't a one-time achievement—it's a mindset, a daily habit of curiosity, experimentation, and continuous improvement. Whether it's refining existing systems or developing disruptive technologies, consistent innovation ensures you remain a valuable contributor in your field.

Being pushed aside in technology doesn't happen suddenly—it creeps in when you become complacent. One day, you may realize that your skills are outdated, your ideas are no longer relevant, and the market has moved on without you. To prevent this, you must invest in your growth, stay informed about industry developments, and surround yourself with others who challenge you to think differently. Innovation is the engine that drives technology forward, and those who commit to it not only survive but thrive in a field where change is the only constant.

79. THROUGH THE LENS OF MONEY

One stormy night, a powerful wind snapped a large tree that stood right on the border of Joe's property. The tree, however, belonged to his neighbors, Ted and Debra. It crashed into Joe's yard, damaging part of his landscaping and creating a mess of broken branches and a massive fallen trunk. For two weeks, the tree remained untouched. Joe waited patiently, assuming his neighbors would take the initiative to remove it. But as the days passed with no action, Joe began to feel uncertain about his next steps. Not wanting to create conflict, he decided to do some research before approaching Ted and Debra.

After reviewing local property and liability laws, Joe discovered that when a tree falls due to a natural event such as a storm—legally considered an "act of God"—the property owner where the tree lands is responsible for the cleanup, not the owner of the tree. Armed with this knowledge, Joe contacted several tree removal companies and obtained quotes. Before proceeding with the job, he reached out to Ted and Debra to inform them of his plan to have the tree removed. Ted, caught off guard but relieved, offered to pay half of the removal costs. Joe appreciated the gesture and moved forward with hiring the most reasonably priced company.

The next day, as the tree removal crew arrived with two trucks and heavy equipment to haul and chip the massive log, Debra suddenly appeared, confronting Joe in front of the workers. She accused the crew of overcharging, despite the fact that their quote was significantly lower than other companies Joe had contacted. The crew, visibly frustrated, pointed out that the job involved substantial labor and equipment, and their profit margin was minimal. Joe quickly realized what was happening—Debra's sudden protest was likely an attempt to avoid paying the agreed share of the cost. While the job was completed professionally, the incident left Joe with a clearer understanding of his neighbors' intentions and a lesson in how good intentions can sometimes be taken for granted.

Money has a remarkable way of uncovering the true nature of people. When times are good and no financial tension exists, relationships may appear smooth and friendly. However, the moment money becomes involved—especially when someone owes you—it often reveals unexpected sides of their character. People who once seemed trustworthy and kind may begin to avoid conversations, delay responses, or create elaborate excuses to postpone repayment. These moments test the strength of integrity and honesty, showing whether someone values responsibility or prefers to hide behind justifications.

When people owe money and fail to take accountability, it's rarely about the amount—it's about their priorities and respect for others. Excuses such as forgotten bills, unexpected emergencies, or delayed paychecks may occasionally be valid, but repeated patterns often point to avoidance and a lack of maturity. True character is shown when someone communicates openly, takes ownership, and honors their word, even under financial pressure. Conversely, those who dodge obligations reveal a self-serving mindset, placing their convenience above fairness. In this way, money becomes more than just currency—it becomes a lens through which loyalty, integrity, and respect are clearly seen.

80. SETBACKS TO BUILDING EMPIRES

After years of consultations, negotiations, and the struggle to secure financing, a small town in a small country finally succeeded in building a bridge across the mighty river. The new crossing transformed daily life—shortening distances, boosting trade, and fueling growth. Businesses flourished, new opportunities arose, and the once-quiet town began to expand with renewed confidence and prosperity.

But misfortune struck when a powerful earthquake reduced the bridge to rubble. Instead of despair, the town found strength in unity. City leaders and local enterprises pooled their resources, worked tirelessly, and within months a new bridge rose in place of the old one. The rapid rebuilding became a symbol of resilience and determination, reminding the townspeople that even in the face of disaster, progress could be restored.

At times, our professional lives or business ventures encounter setbacks that may feel overwhelming and discouraging. Projects fail, opportunities slip away, or unforeseen circumstances interrupt progress, leaving us questioning our abilities and direction. Yet these challenges are not the end of the journey but rather part of the process that shapes resilience, creativity, and determination.

What matters most during such moments is our response. By working diligently, remaining disciplined, and refusing to lose hope, we create the foundation for recovery and future success. Every small effort, even when it feels unnoticed, builds momentum. Over time, persistence turns obstacles into stepping stones, and lessons from failure become tools that strengthen our strategies for the future.

History and everyday life alike show us that great achievements often emerge from adversity. Many mighty enterprises, enduring careers, and lasting legacies have been built by individuals who refused to surrender when faced with difficulty. With patience, focus, and unwavering faith in one's vision, it is possible not only to recover but to rise higher than before, building an "empire" of success more quickly and powerfully than one might have imagined.

81. INFLUENCE

Chocolates are cherished worldwide, enjoyed by people of all ages for their rich taste and comforting sweetness. The journey of chocolate begins with the cocoa bean, which is carefully removed from its protective pod. These beans are then gathered and left to undergo fermentation, a crucial natural step that transforms their flavor profile. After fermentation, the beans are dried to remove excess moisture and roasted to release the deep, complex aromas that make chocolate so irresistible. Each of these steps plays a vital role in creating the final product, ensuring the smooth texture and distinct flavor we associate with fine chocolate.

What makes this process even more fascinating is the influence of the natural microbiome present on each cocoa farm. Fermentation typically occurs without the need for added microbes, relying instead on the unique microbial community that thrives in the local environment. These microbes break down the pulp surrounding the beans, releasing chemical compounds that shape the flavor and aroma of the chocolate. Farms with diverse and balanced microbiomes often produce beans that yield superior-tasting chocolate, while poor microbial balance can result in less desirable flavors. Thus, the richness of chocolate is not only a result of careful human craftsmanship but also the invisible work of nature itself.

Just as the finest chocolates come from farms that nurture a healthy and diverse microbiome, our own lives are also shaped by the environment and influences around us. From the moment we are born, we begin absorbing lessons, behaviors, and values from the people closest to us. Parents, siblings, and relatives play an especially important role in setting the foundation of who we are, guiding us with their words, actions, and choices. Just as a cocoa bean cannot develop into chocolate without proper fermentation, we too cannot grow into our fullest selves without the nurturing influences of those who surround us.

Beyond family, friends, teachers, and mentors also leave a lasting mark on our personalities and decisions. Their encouragement, criticism, or even casual remarks can shape the way we see ourselves and the world. Even the art and media we consume—whether it be movies, books, music, or social platforms—quietly mold our perspectives and aspirations. Each influence acts like a different "microbe" in our personal fermentation process, contributing to the flavor of our character. Some influences add sweetness, patience, or wisdom, while others may bring bitterness, impatience, or doubt.

Ultimately, just as the best-tasting chocolate depends on a farm's healthy microbiome, the best version of ourselves emerges when we are surrounded by positive, inspiring, and balanced influences. By carefully choosing the people we allow into our inner circles and the content we feed our minds, we can shape our conduct, values, and vision for life in a way that enriches both ourselves and those around us. The quality of our character, like the quality of chocolate, is the product of both nature and nurture working in harmony.

82. FORGED THROUGH STRUGGLES

A soldier in an elite force undergoes much more rigorous training than a regular soldier, starting with early mornings filled with intense physical activity such as walking, running, and jumping while carrying heavy loads and weapons. Their training often includes pushing, carrying, or flipping large tires to build strength and endurance. After months or even years of this demanding preparation, they are fully equipped to confront terrorists and other threats to society.

Sometimes, life feels unbearably heavy, throwing challenges our way that seem unfair or never-ending. We may question why certain hardships come to us while others appear to move through life effortlessly. The weight of setbacks, failures, and difficult circumstances can leave us drained, frustrated, and even doubtful about our own abilities. Yet, within these struggles lies a silent test of patience, courage, and perseverance, shaping us in ways that we often do not realize in the moment.

In many situations, we are required to push ourselves harder than those around us. Some people may glide by with fewer obstacles, while we are left working extra hours, juggling multiple responsibilities, or forcing ourselves to step into uncomfortable, unfamiliar territory.

The road can feel long and lonely, progress may appear invisible, and the sense of being "behind" can gnaw at our confidence. However, it is precisely this extra effort—the sweat, the sacrifice, the persistence—that lays the foundation for something greater. Every step forward, no matter how small, becomes part of a hidden strength that others may never see.

What if the trials we face are not roadblocks but stepping stones? Just like an athlete builds endurance through grueling training, our hardships may be refining us for a purpose beyond our current understanding. The lessons learned in struggle—resilience, empathy, determination—are priceless qualities that cannot be developed in comfort. One day, the pieces may come together, and we'll see that the challenges we endured were preparing us to rise higher than we ever imagined. Life's toughest moments might, in fact, be the very ones carving out the greatness within us.

83. ADAPTING YOUR MINDSET FOR NON-ROUTINE CHALLENGES

Ben was a dedicated professor at a community college located in a struggling neighborhood. Teaching was more than a profession for him—it was a calling. He poured his heart into guiding students, many of whom came from difficult backgrounds. Beyond lectures and assignments, Ben listened to their problems, encouraged their dreams, and reminded them that education was a way to rise above hardship. His compassion and humility made him more than a teacher; to many, he was a mentor, a counselor, and even a father figure.

One day, Ben decided it was time to part with his old car. The vehicle was still in working condition, but the upkeep was draining his limited resources. Despite knowing it had more value, he quoted a price far below its worth. To Ben, the car was not just an object of sale but a way to help someone else who might need affordable transportation. For him, the decision was guided less by profit and more by his natural generosity, reflecting the same spirit of selflessness he carried into his classroom. The buyer recognized the bargain immediately and happily accepted the offer. Later, he resold the car at a much higher price, walking away with a sizable profit.

When faced with a non-routine job, the first step is to recognize that it demands a different way of thinking. Routine work often relies on habit, structure, and repetition, but unfamiliar challenges require adaptability and creativity. You must be willing to step outside your comfort zone, question old patterns, and develop fresh approaches that suit the situation. A flexible mindset opens the door to problem-solving, innovation, and ultimately success in tasks that do not follow the usual path.

Equally important is understanding the distinction between different environments, particularly when moving between non-profit work and business ventures. In a non-profit setting, decisions are often guided by service, compassion, and community benefit. However, in business, the focus shifts toward sustainability, growth, and profitability. Carrying the same mindset from one environment into the other can create inefficiencies and missed opportunities. To thrive, you must consciously adjust your perspective and align it with the goals of the task at hand.

This shift in thinking is not about abandoning values but about applying them wisely in context. A business run with the mindset of a charity may struggle to survive, just as a non-profit run with the mindset of pure profit may lose its purpose. Success comes from clarity—

knowing when to be compassionate and service-oriented, and when to be strategic, competitive, and profit-driven. By learning to adapt your mindset, you prepare yourself not only to handle non-routine jobs but also to grow as a professional capable of navigating diverse challenges.

84. THE CAUTION OF GIVING

Walter was an amateur photographer with a passion for experimenting with different settings and props. One afternoon, he decided to capture the beauty of the beach. To add a touch of creativity, he purchased a few souvenir starfish from a nearby shop and carefully placed them in the sand as part of his composition, blending them into the natural scenery.

As Walter focused on his work, a group of children playing nearby grew curious and gathered around to watch. Once he finished taking pictures, the children eagerly asked if they could have the starfish. At first, Walter hesitated—after all, they were his chosen props and held some value to him. But seeing the children's excitement and persistence, he relented and handed over his treasured souvenirs.

The children proudly carried the starfish to their car as their family prepared for the long four-hour drive home. Along the way, the children fell asleep, leaving the starfish forgotten on the floor of the vehicle. When they finally arrived home late that night, their tired parents, noticing the neglected trinkets, casually tossed them into the trash, ending the journey of Walter's once-prized souvenirs.

When you choose to give something to someone—whether it is a book, money, or even an opportunity—there is no assurance that it will be valued or handled with care. A book that you treasured and loaned out in good faith may never find its way back to your shelf. Money lent with trust and good intention can often be delayed in repayment, or in some cases, not returned at all. Even when you recommend someone for a job, their lack of commitment or laziness may reflect poorly on you rather than them. Such experiences remind us that generosity does not always guarantee responsibility from the receiver.

These disappointments arise from the simple truth that people think and act differently. What you value and nurture may not carry the same weight in another person's eyes. While you may see the importance of honoring promises and respecting others' belongings, others might treat these matters casually. This difference in perspective can lead to frustration, especially when your goodwill is not reciprocated with the same level of care or accountability.

Therefore, it is wise to pause and reflect before offering help. This does not mean closing your heart to others, but rather approaching generosity with discernment. Think carefully about who you choose to trust, and understand that once something leaves your hands, you may have little control over its fate. Being cautious in how you extend help allows you to protect yourself from unnecessary disappointment, while still leaving room for kindness when it is truly deserved.

85. PARENTAL PROTECTION HAS ITS LIMITS

The suburban houses were admired not just for their carefully designed architecture but also for the lawns that surrounded them, adding vibrancy and charm. At the center of one such yard stood a tall tree whose wide canopy provided shade from the blazing sun. Beneath it, the grass appeared especially lush and green, its freshness seemingly a gift from the tree's protection. The shaded grass often seemed to mock the shorter blades growing at the edges, unaware that those smaller, less vibrant blades had developed deeper and longer root systems in order to draw water from the ground.

One summer, however, a fierce storm swept through the town. The mighty tree that had once sheltered the lawn collapsed under the force of the winds, leaving the grass beneath it suddenly exposed. As if the storm alone were not enough, a drought soon followed, parching the soil and draining the last drops of surface moisture. In response to the scarcity of water, the government imposed restrictions, forbidding homeowners from watering their lawns to conserve resources.

Without the protection of the tree's shade and lacking the resilience to survive on its own, the once healthy and enviable lawn grass shriveled and died. In contrast, the small blades that had always been overlooked endured, their deep roots reaching far underground to access hidden reserves of water. What had once seemed a weakness turned into their greatest strength, proving that true survival often depends not on outward appearances but on unseen foundations built over time.

Children born into wealthy families often inherit not only financial security but also opportunities that can open many doors in life. However, wealth alone does not guarantee lasting success. If these children fail to use their resources wisely, they may struggle to sustain the prosperity they were born into. Education, discipline, and a sense of responsibility are critical, for without them, wealth can quickly slip away.

The dangers are many when privilege is not matched with wisdom. Poor education leaves children ill-equipped to manage businesses, estates, or even their own personal finances. Bad friendships can lead them into destructive habits or exploitative relationships that drain their resources. Likewise, arrogance, entitlement, or careless behavior can damage reputations and erode the foundation upon which their families built their success.

While parents are alive, such children may continue to enjoy the benefits of wealth and protection, often shielded from the consequences of their actions. Yet, when their parents pass away, they face the reality of standing on their own. Without the discipline to manage their inheritance, they may squander it, while those who cultivated wisdom, humility, and perseverance often thrive. True success, then, depends not on inherited riches but on the character and choices made by each individual.

86. LIFE IS NOT A POPULARITY CONTEST

Scientific and technical journals often have limited circulation, as their primary audience consists of researchers, scientists, engineers, and professionals directly involved in these fields. Unlike popular magazines or mainstream media, these journals are not designed for mass appeal. Their language is technical, their content is highly specialized, and their readership is usually restricted to those with the expertise to fully understand and apply the information. Because of this, the average person may not encounter these journals in daily life, leading to the perception that they are unimportant or irrelevant outside the scientific community.

However, this perception is far from true. Scientific and technical journals play a crucial role in shaping the future by publishing groundbreaking discoveries and innovative technologies that eventually impact everyone. From medical breakthroughs that save lives, to advancements in communication, energy, and transportation, nearly every modern convenience traces its roots to knowledge first shared in these journals. What begins as specialized research eventually becomes the foundation for new products, services, and solutions that transform the way societies function. Thus, while the journals themselves may not be widely read, the knowledge they contain ripples outward, influencing industries, governments, and ultimately the daily lives of people across the globe.

Life is not meant to be a popularity contest, even though society often makes it seem that way. Many people equate success or happiness with being well-liked, admired, or recognized by large groups of people. However, true value in life is not measured by the number of friends, followers, or compliments one receives. Instead, it is reflected in the quiet, meaningful ways we contribute to the lives of others and the integrity with which we carry ourselves. Popularity may come and go, but character and kindness leave a much deeper and lasting impression.

You may not be the most popular person in your office, school, or social circle, but that does not mean your presence goes unnoticed. Sometimes, a single act of kindness, a helpful word, a smile, or even the way you carry out your responsibilities can inspire or uplift others in ways you never realize. A colleague may learn diligence from your work ethic, a friend may find comfort in your patience, or a stranger may feel valued because of your respect. These quiet contributions often matter far more than fleeting popularity, because they shape the values, attitudes, and confidence of those around you.

In fact, the greatest impact we have on others is often invisible to us. You may never know whose perspective you have changed, whose burdens you have lightened, or whose path you have influenced simply by being yourself. Popularity seeks recognition, but true influence does not require applause. It thrives in sincerity, humility, and consistency. By focusing less on being admired and more on being authentic and kind, you may end up touching more lives than the most popular person ever could—leaving behind a legacy of meaning rather than just a memory of charm.

87. LEADERSHIP THROUGH EXAMPLE AND SUPPORT

From the moment baby Stan came home from the hospital, a golden retriever named Tigu became his inseparable companion. Tigu was more than just a pet; he acted as Stan's guardian, never allowing strangers to come too close to the infant. As Stan grew older, the two formed a bond that was almost brotherly. They slept in the same bed, shared food at the table, and spent nearly every moment together. Their companionship was so touching that videos of their interactions gained widespread attention and admiration on social media, capturing the essence of pure loyalty and love between a boy and his dog.

Years later, life brought inevitable change. Tigu passed away, leaving Stan with cherished memories and an unshakable sense of loyalty that the dog had taught him. As Stan grew into adulthood, he pursued a career in the army and was assigned to a unit that lacked structure and suffered from high turnover. Drawing on the lessons of devotion and care he learned from Tigu, Stan chose not to distance himself with the rigid airs of an officer. Instead, he led with humility and empathy— eating meals alongside his men, occasionally sleeping in the same barracks, and training shoulder-to-shoulder with them. In time, his approach earned him genuine respect and trust from those under his command.

That bond of trust proved invaluable when Stan's unit was deployed overseas into the harsh realities of war. Unlike other units that required constant orders and supervision, his men operated as a cohesive force, each soldier understanding his role and carrying it out with discipline and commitment. Stan's leadership, rooted in the lessons of loyalty, protection, and companionship once embodied by Tigu, transformed the unit into a dependable, resilient team. In many ways, the spirit of his golden retriever still lived on— guiding Stan as he protected and led others with the same devotion Tigu had once shown him.

True leadership is not merely about holding a title or giving orders—it is about gaining the trust and support of subordinates and colleagues. A leader who earns respect rather than demands it is able to inspire commitment and loyalty within the team. When people feel valued, heard, and guided with fairness, they are far more willing to put forth their best efforts. Support from subordinates becomes the foundation of success, as it creates an environment where collaboration thrives and collective goals are achieved more effectively.

At the heart of effective leadership lies the responsibility to be a role model. A leader's actions speak louder than their words, and when they demonstrate integrity, dedication, and accountability, others are naturally encouraged to emulate those qualities. Whether it is meeting deadlines, facing challenges with courage, or treating everyone with dignity, the leader sets the standard for the team. People tend to mirror what they observe, so if they see their leader consistently displaying discipline and commitment, they are more inclined to adopt the same mindset and behaviors.

Equally important is the leader's ability to work alongside their subordinates rather than above them. When a leader is willing to put in the same effort, endure the same hardships, and celebrate the same victories as their team, they cultivate a spirit of unity. Subordinates begin to view the leader not as a distant authority figure but as a guiding force who genuinely cares about shared success. This approach not only strengthens morale but also fosters a culture of mutual respect and accountability, where every individual feels motivated to contribute their best. In this way, true leadership is built on example, support, and the ability to inspire through action.

88. VALUE FOR MONEY

Carlson was the only son of an affluent family, and from childhood he had grown accustomed to comfort and luxury. His parents provided for all his needs, and he never had to worry about expenses. When he entered college, however, his father began to notice that Carlson was spending money recklessly—lavish outings, extravagant purchases, and no regard for savings. It was clear to his father that Carlson had no understanding of the value of money, and unless something was done, he would continue down a careless path.

At the end of his first year of college, Carlson returned home for summer break. Expecting another season of leisure, he was stunned when his father informed him of a different plan. Carlson was to spend the summer working for Farmer Jim, a man known for running a tough but honest farm. Carlson protested, hesitant and reluctant to give up his comforts. His father, however, was firm: unless Carlson agreed to this, he would not continue to pay for his college expenses. Faced with no other choice, Carlson reluctantly packed his bags and reported to the farm.

Farmer Jim's farm employed close to a hundred workers during the summer. The work was relentless—planting quick-growing vegetables, harvesting them at peak time, and sorting them for sale. The blazing sun beat down mercilessly, and breaks were scarce. Carlson, who had never known such exhaustion, struggled to keep up with the pace. He soon discovered that even after enduring long hours, the workers were given only the minimum wages fixed by the government. To add to his surprise, he was placed in the employee quarters and charged for rent, meals, and utilities, just like everyone else.

For the first time in his life, Carlson was forced to balance earnings against expenses. Every dollar mattered, and he realized that the money he earned through sweat and effort disappeared quickly once basic needs were covered. Gone were the days of carefree spending; now he carefully counted every coin, ensuring he had enough for food and shelter. The hardships also gave him newfound respect for the farmhands, men and women who endured this grueling life year after year to provide for their families. Slowly, the lessons of responsibility, discipline, and gratitude began to take root in his heart.

When Carlson returned home after 100 days of labor, he was no longer the same young man. The pampered, careless spender had grown into someone who understood the value of work and the dignity of money earned through effort. He approached his finances with caution and maturity, no longer wasting resources on luxuries. His father saw the transformation and knew the lesson had taken hold. The summer at Farmer Jim's farm had been the making of Carlson, teaching him life skills no classroom or privilege could provide.

89. THE MUSICAL CHAIR OF GOVERNANCE: CLEANING UP AFTER THE LAST TUNE

Stephanie is a typical high school teenager who, despite constant reminders, consistently neglects one particular chore—cleaning her room. Every morning before she heads out to school, her mother, Ms. Lucy, gently or sometimes firmly reminds her to tidy up her space. However, Stephanie rarely takes the request seriously and leaves her room in disarray without a second thought. Ms. Lucy, who takes pride in maintaining a clean and orderly home, finds it difficult to ignore the mess. Once Stephanie is out the door, she reluctantly steps into her daughter's room and begins the familiar routine of picking up clothes, organizing scattered belongings, and restoring some sense of order. While she doesn't enjoy cleaning up after her daughter, she can't bear to let the room stay in such a chaotic state. Yet, despite Ms. Lucy's quiet efforts and the clean room Stephanie returns to each day, nothing changes. As soon as she's back home, Stephanie resumes her usual habits—dropping her bag on the floor, leaving clothes strewn about, and ignoring the cleanliness her mother worked so hard to restore. The cycle continues, day after day, with Ms. Lucy quietly tidying up and Stephanie remaining oblivious or indifferent to the effort behind the order she takes for granted.

When new governments are elected, there is often great hope and expectation from the public that they will bring positive change and progress. However, not all governments live up to these expectations. Some end up creating significant problems during their time in office. These issues can include a breakdown of law and order, where crime increases and justice systems become ineffective or politicized. Financial indiscipline may also take root, with reckless spending, mismanagement of public funds, and unsustainable borrowing. Corruption can become rampant, with public officials using their positions for personal gain rather than public service. Additionally, such governments may fail to generate employment opportunities, leading to widespread joblessness, and they often neglect critical infrastructure, resulting in deteriorating roads, public facilities, and utilities. The absence of a solid industrial base further worsens the economy, limiting opportunities for investment, innovation, and economic growth.

Once such a government is voted out of office, the incoming administration often faces a daunting task. It must work to clean up the mess left behind and undo the damage caused by its predecessor. This involves restoring order in society, ensuring that institutions function properly, and rebuilding public trust in the system. Economically, the new government may need to impose strict financial controls to stabilize the budget, reduce debt, and manage public resources more responsibly. Tackling corruption becomes a top priority, requiring institutional reforms, stricter enforcement, and sometimes prosecution of past offenders. On the job front, policies must be introduced to stimulate employment and revitalize key sectors of the economy. The task is not only to reverse harmful policies but also to introduce sustainable systems that will prevent similar problems in the future.

Furthermore, rebuilding physical infrastructure and laying the foundation for industrial growth are essential for long-term recovery. This includes investing in roads, power supply, schools, hospitals, and communication networks, while also creating an environment that encourages private sector development and innovation. The new government often inherits a deeply frustrated and skeptical population, making public engagement and transparency crucial for restoring confidence. These efforts take time, resources, and political will, and while progress can be slow, responsible leadership can gradually steer a nation back on course. Ultimately, the cycle highlights the importance of accountability and responsible governance, as the failures of one administration inevitably become the burden of the next.

90. THE HOLLOW LEGACY OF SELF GLORY

After serving two successful terms, the mayor stepped down from office, leaving behind a city transformed. His leadership had been marked by a relentless crackdown on crime and lawlessness, which restored public confidence and safety. As the city grew more stable, it began to attract major businesses, with several new companies setting up offices and contributing to a revitalized local economy. The outgoing mayor's vision and dedication created a legacy of law and order, and his chosen successor — someone he had personally mentored — took up the reins with a promise to maintain the progress. For a time, the city's upward trajectory continued, fueled by responsible governance and a commitment to public welfare.

However, years later, a new administration took power under a mayor with very different priorities. Unlike his predecessors, this leader was driven less by public service and more by a desire for fame, influence, and personal enrichment. Eager to win popular support quickly, he rolled out a series of flashy free public services, funding them by imposing heavy taxes on the very companies that had once powered the city's growth. Many businesses, burdened by the new policies, relocated elsewhere. In their absence, unemployment surged, and the city began to deteriorate. Squatters occupied abandoned buildings, crime and corruption resurged, and the city that was once a symbol of order spiraled into chaos. The final blow came as tourists and investors alike turned away, leaving behind a shell of what had once been a thriving urban success story.

Some individuals pursue positions of office not out of a genuine desire to serve, but rather to elevate their own image and status. They see leadership as a platform for personal glorification, using the authority entrusted to them as a tool to command admiration and power. Instead of prioritizing the responsibilities that come with their role, they focus on building a façade of greatness, seeking recognition and praise at the expense of those they are meant to represent.

In many cases, such leaders exploit their positions for personal gain. They accumulate wealth, benefits, and privileges while neglecting the very communities that placed their trust in them. Their decisions are often guided by self-interest rather than the common good, and over time, this leads to corruption, inequality, and a loss of public faith in leadership. Rather than uplifting society, they deepen the divide between themselves and the people they are supposed to serve.

Ultimately, the legacy of such individuals is one of disappointment and failure. History remembers them not for noble contributions, but for the greed and selfishness that defined their time in power. While they may taste temporary success and bask in fleeting admiration, their names inevitably become linked to the suffering, setbacks, and disillusionment they left behind. What remains of their lives is not honor but emptiness, for a legacy built on self-glory always crumbles. Greatness does not endure in possessions, titles, or monuments, but in the good one imparts to others. Those who enter office seeking to glorify themselves may accumulate wealth and recognition, yet they fail to leave behind meaning. True remembrance belongs only to those who gave more than they received, whose service was rooted in humility, and whose integrity outshone their pride.

91. THE RIGHT TIME TO HARVEST OPPORTUNITIES

Arnold's mother asked him to pick tomatoes from their kitchen garden one afternoon. When Arnold went to check, he saw that the tomatoes were still green and unripe. He returned and explained that they were not ready to be harvested. Trusting his judgment, the tomatoes were left untouched. Two days later, Arnold returned to the garden only to discover that many of the ripe tomatoes had already been eaten by birds and rodents. What could have been enjoyed fresh and whole was now spoiled, leaving behind only a few good ones to be saved.

Disappointed but determined not to waste what remained, Arnold picked the tomatoes that were still partially ripe. He placed them in the kitchen, and within a few days, they naturally ripened. Although the family could still enjoy them, Arnold realized that if he had acted earlier, they might have had more tomatoes and avoided losing so many to nature. This small incident left him with a larger lesson: timing is everything, and hesitation often leads to missed opportunities.

The story of the tomatoes reflects a greater truth about life. When people graduate from college, learn new skills, or discover talents within themselves, they should not wait too long to put them to use. Just as Arnold's hesitation allowed the best tomatoes to be eaten away, delaying the pursuit of one's goals can give doubt, fear, and missed chances the opportunity to steal away potential. Whether it is a career, a passion, or a dream, waiting too long often means that the best moment passes by.

For those who are gifted—whether in academics, arts, or other talents—the key is to act with courage and seize opportunities as they arise. The longer one delays, the more room there is for self-doubt to creep in and erode confidence. Just as the partially ripe tomatoes eventually ripened indoors, one can still recover and succeed later in life. But to harvest the fullest rewards, it is always better to act when the time is right, before circumstances or hesitation cause opportunities to slip away.

92. KINGS, QUEENS AND SLAVES OF THE HEART

Long ago, kings and queens were revered almost as divine beings, often regarded as representatives of the gods on earth. Their authority was absolute, and they wielded the power to make decisions that shaped the destiny of their kingdoms without question. Subjects bowed to them with deep respect, not only out of loyalty but also from fear of incurring their wrath, which could bring severe punishment or disgrace. At the same time, rulers were expected to provide protection, ensure justice, and maintain order, which created a bond of dependence between the monarchs and their people. Those employed in the royal court, from soldiers to servants, were sustained by the wealth of the kingdom, receiving care, provisions, and payment for their services. This system reinforced the king's or queen's position as the central figure of society, embodying both power and responsibility in the eyes of their subjects.

Kingdoms, with their grandeur and absolute monarchs, have largely vanished into the pages of history, though some remnants of royalty and traditional rule still remain in certain regions, particularly in the Middle East. While the political power of kings and queens has faded, the imagery of royalty continues to live on in our everyday language and relationships.

The idea of treating someone as a king or queen is often used as a metaphor for respect, honor, and care, showing how the ancient reverence for royalty still shapes the way we express love and admiration today.

In families, this symbolism often comes alive. A husband may treat his wife like a queen, ensuring she feels cherished, valued, and respected, while a wife may treat her husband like a king, offering support, love, and loyalty. Children, too, may elevate their parents to a royal status in their own eyes, seeing them as protectors, providers, and guiding figures who deserve reverence. In such settings, the idea of royalty becomes less about power and control, and more about mutual appreciation and acknowledgment of each other's importance in daily life.

However, when love and respect are replaced by bitterness or resentment, the metaphor can quickly shift. Instead of treating one another like kings and queens, people may reduce each other to the status of slaves—dominated, disrespected, or taken for granted. This shift reflects the fragility of relationships when they are not nurtured with care. Ultimately, whether in kingdoms of the past or in families of the present, the true strength of any bond lies in how people choose to treat one another: with dignity and kindness, or with disregard and hostility.

93. SHINING THROUGH ADVERSITY

Borg was an accomplished sportsman whose dedication and talent earned him numerous medals and trophies over the years. Proud of his achievements, he displayed these awards prominently in a glass showcase at home, where each piece told a story of hard work and triumph. The collection included solid bronze medals and several gold-plated trophies, all of which shimmered under the light. Every year, without fail, Borg would carefully remove each item, clean it meticulously, and restore its original shine, a ritual that reflected his deep respect for the journey behind every award. Friends and family who visited were always impressed by how pristine and well-preserved the display remained—many remarked that the medals looked as if they had just been awarded, a testament not only to Borg's athletic excellence but also to the care with which he honored his legacy.

There are times in life—often when you are respected, well-known, and carry yourself with dignity—when you may find yourself unexpectedly targeted. Despite your good conduct and integrity, others may seek to tarnish your name. Whether out of jealousy, resentment, or personal vendettas, some individuals may resort to spreading falsehoods, misrepresenting your actions, or questioning your intentions. These moments can feel deeply unfair, especially when you've worked hard to build a reputation grounded in honesty and respect.

When faced with such attacks, it's important to remain anchored in the truth. You may be tempted to retaliate or defend yourself loudly, but often the most powerful response is to continue living in alignment with your values. The truth has a quiet strength—it doesn't always need to shout to be heard. Even when others doubt you or try to drag your name through the mud, maintaining your composure and staying grounded in who you are can speak volumes. Let your actions continue to reflect your character, and trust that in time, lies lose their grip while the truth endures.

In the end, your reputation—though momentarily clouded—can emerge brighter than before. Like metal polished after weathering a storm, your name can shine with renewed luster, admired even more for having stood the test of adversity. The journey through slander and struggle often reveals your true strength and resilience. People may eventually see not just the attacks you endured, but the grace and courage with which you faced them. And when that happens, your character won't just be restored—it will glitter.

94. DEMIGODS WITH CLOSED EYES

At a well-known global corporation, the top executives occupied the upper floors of a grand office building, a physical and symbolic separation from the rest of the staff. They enjoyed the luxury of a private elevator, a privilege denied to junior executives and employees. This exclusivity reinforced a culture of hierarchy and distance, where senior leaders kept themselves insulated from the voices below. Employees at lower levels quickly realized that their ideas, insights, and concerns would never reach the ears of those at the top.

The refusal of the senior executives to listen or engage with their workforce created a serious communication gap. While employees on the ground floor and in everyday operations saw problems and opportunities firsthand, they had no way to convey these realities upward. The executives not only ignored suggestions but also discouraged attempts at communication, often treating junior staff with contempt. Over time, this disconnect led the company to drift away from the practical needs and demands of its customers, blinding leadership to the growing issues surrounding product quality and design.

Despite enjoying significant government backing, the company could not withstand the negative impact of poor reviews, flawed product designs, and an increasingly dissatisfied customer base. The leadership's arrogance and refusal to adapt eventually eroded its credibility and market position. After decades of decline, the business that once stood as a giant in its field collapsed entirely, forced into bankruptcy. What could have been avoided through openness and humility became a cautionary tale of how isolation at the top can destroy even the strongest organizations.

In some companies, certain executives have little to no connection with the organization's history, culture, or workforce. They operate with inflated egos, projecting an image of authority while remaining detached from the realities of the workplace. Their behavior is often compared to a balloon floating on nothing but pride, fragile yet untouchable. In such an environment, junior executives and employees are silenced, their ideas dismissed before they can even be voiced. This lack of engagement fosters a culture where people stay only for the paycheck or benefits, and as soon as a better opportunity arises, they leave—leading to high turnover and instability.

When senior executives retire, resign, or are transferred, corporate communications usually send out a formal notice. Yet, these announcements rarely cause any genuine reaction within the company, as most employees feel no personal connection to these leaders. The absence of relationships built on respect or collaboration leaves many indifferent, and in cases where an executive was known for arrogance or hostility, the departure is even met with relief, often summed up by the sentiment, "good riddance." Such moments reveal how little impact these leaders had on the human fabric of the organization.

Outside the company, only family members and neighbors may truly know that someone holds an executive position, because within the workplace itself, these leaders remain practically invisible. Their detachment ensures that employees view them as distant figures, not as approachable mentors or role models. On the other hand, executives who choose to value people, invest in communication, and respect their teams become deeply admired. Their names resonate across the workplace, leaving lasting impressions that outlive their tenure.

True leadership requires humility and openness. Senior executives must recognize that innovation often comes from fresh perspectives, and many junior employees may possess ideas far more valuable than they realize. These ideas will only surface in an environment that encourages dialogue and respects contributions at every level. By fostering a culture of inclusion rather than ego-driven exclusivity, leaders can not only inspire loyalty but also unlock the creativity and energy needed to drive long-term success.

95. THE THEATER OF LIFE: CREATING STORIES WORTH WATCHING

We often find ourselves uninterested in movies that recycle the same storyline. When the plot is predictable and the characters are too familiar, the magic of storytelling is lost. What makes cinema, books, or even a simple tale memorable is its originality—the spark of creativity that sets it apart from what came before. Just as audiences yearn for something new, life itself demands uniqueness in the roles we play.

Each of us is a character shaped by the era in which we live. Our personalities, choices, and actions form a script, and the people around us become part of the performance. Sometimes they applaud, sometimes they criticize, but their reactions are part of the unfolding drama. No two people live the same exact life, even if the circumstances seem similar. It is our distinctiveness, the way we embody our roles, that makes our existence meaningful.

Yet, there is an ultimate audience beyond the people around us—God. Every act, word, and gesture is witnessed by Him. Just as a discerning viewer would not enjoy a repetitive film, God too takes delight in seeing variety, sincerity, and creativity in the stories of our lives. He does not call for imitation or monotony but for authenticity, innovation, and genuine expression. Our lives are not meant to be copies of others but original works of art performed before the highest spectator.

Therefore, it is important to embrace life as an opportunity to create something new. Be original in thought, be creative in action, and live with diligence and purpose. Do not simply repeat what has already been done by others; instead, add your unique voice to the grand narrative of existence. In doing so, you not only engage those around you but also honor the Creator who has given you the stage and entrusted you with a role that only you can play.

96. BLENDING MANAGEMENT AND SPIRIT FOR LASTING PROJECT SUCCESS

When enjoying a meal, the experience often comes not from consuming each ingredient in isolation but from the harmony created when they are combined. For instance, when eating a burger, no one usually separates the bun, the patty, the cheese, the lettuce, the tomato, and the condiments to eat them one at a time; instead, the pleasure lies in taking a bite that brings all those flavors and textures together in a balanced, satisfying way. The same principle applies when eating rice with various side dishes—vegetables, meats, or curries are not meant to be eaten completely apart from the rice but rather mixed in, allowing the grains to absorb the sauces and flavors of the sides so that each bite becomes a blend of tastes and aromas. This method of eating reflects not just culinary preference but also cultural traditions across the world, where the act of combining foods represents the idea that the whole is greater than the sum of its parts.

When undertaking any project, it is important to recognize that success does not rely solely on technical execution or organizational skills. There are two deeply interconnected aspects that play a role in shaping the outcome: the management component and the spiritual component. The management side encompasses planning, structuring, allocating resources, meeting deadlines, and ensuring that all parts of the project align efficiently. This is the visible framework that determines how well tasks are coordinated and completed. However, beyond these logistical elements, there exists the spiritual component, which reflects the values, motivations, energy, and sense of purpose that people bring to the work. Together, these two aspects are woven into the fabric of any meaningful endeavor.

The spiritual component, though less tangible, is no less powerful. It represents the belief, inspiration, and passion that breathe life into a project. When individuals are guided by a strong sense of purpose, they infuse their work with creativity, resilience, and dedication. This inner drive often becomes the force that carries a project through obstacles and uncertainties, allowing people to remain motivated even in the face of setbacks. Without this underlying spirit, management techniques alone can feel mechanical or hollow, lacking the human depth and emotional investment needed to transform a project into something remarkable. It is the spiritual dimension that keeps people united, inspired, and determined to see their goals through.

Ultimately, the most successful projects are those where management and spirit are not separated but harmoniously blended. Just as a meal is enjoyed when flavors are mixed together, a project thrives when structure and soul are combined in balance. Management provides the discipline and order to move steadily forward, while the spiritual component provides the heart and vision that make the journey meaningful. When these two forces are intertwined, the outcome is not only efficient and well-executed but also fulfilling, memorable, and impactful for everyone involved. This integration of both practical and spiritual elements ensures that a project does not just end well but also creates a lasting sense of accomplishment and shared purpose.

97. KEEPING THE FAITH WHIILE PASSING THROUGH THE STORM

In the Old Testament's Book of Job, we find the story of a man who faced unimaginable loss and suffering. Job was a prosperous and righteous man, blessed with great wealth and a large, loving family. However, in a series of devastating events, he lost all his possessions and his children. Despite his grief and confusion, Job remained steadfast in his faith. Rather than curse God as many would have, he humbly declared, "The Lord gave, and the Lord has taken away; blessed be the name of the Lord." His words reflected deep spiritual conviction and trust in a higher purpose, even when circumstances were cruel and unjust.

Job's suffering was made worse by those closest to him. His wife urged him to abandon his faith, and his friends wrongly insisted that his misfortune must be the result of his own sin. Yet, Job refused to turn his back on God. Instead of harboring resentment, he prayed for his friends, showing humility and grace. In the end, God honored Job's faith and integrity. Not only was his health restored, but everything he had lost was returned to him in greater measure—his wealth was multiplied, and he was blessed with a new family and long life. Job's story is a powerful reminder that unwavering faith through hardship can lead to restoration and blessings beyond what was originally lost.

There are moments in life when everything seems to fall apart—when we lose our health, wealth, our family, or our reputation. These losses can feel unbearable, stripping away our sense of identity and stability. In such dark times, many people find it difficult to cope. Some turn to alcohol or gambling in search of temporary escape, while others, in their deepest despair, may even consider ending their lives. These reactions, though human, often deepen the pain and prolong the journey toward healing. The truth is, no one is immune to hardship, and life can change drastically without warning.

However, life is not a straight path, and setbacks do not define our final destination. Even the most successful individuals have faced severe trials and passed through tight, uncomfortable bottlenecks where everything felt hopeless. What sets them apart is not the absence of difficulty, but the presence of perseverance and unwavering faith. They held on to the belief that there was purpose in their pain and strength to be gained through their struggle. Rather than surrendering to fear or despair, they kept moving forward, often clinging to hope even when it was hard to see.

In times of hardship, the most powerful thing you can do is to keep your faith alive. Hold on to your trust in God, even when the road is dark and unclear. Believe that your story is not over and that something greater lies ahead. Faith doesn't promise an easy journey, but it assures a meaningful one. When you remain anchored in the Lord, even your greatest losses can become the soil in which your greatest blessings grow. In the end, with patience and perseverance, you will not only survive—you will succeed.

98. BUILDING THE HOUSE ON SAND

In Matthew 7:24–27, Jesus shares a powerful parable about two men—one who built his house on a rock, and another who built his house on sand. When the rains came, the wind blew, and floods rose, the house built on the rock stood firm, while the one built on sand collapsed with a great crash. This parable is a metaphor about the foundation of one's life. A person who builds their life on solid values— truth, faith, integrity—is like the man who builds on rock. Those who live superficially, without grounding in moral or spiritual principles, are like the man who builds on sand—vulnerable to collapse when hardship comes.

In today's world, people are earning more than any generation in human history. With economic progress and globalization, a wide range of high-paying jobs are available, and the modern workforce is compensated generously across many industries. But along with this rise in income, there has also been a parallel explosion in luxury consumerism. The market is flooded with high-end goods—from expensive clothing and watches to gourmet foods and exclusive travel experiences—that cater to the desire for indulgence and status.

This increase in wealth has also given rise to a culture of display, where living a lavish life is not only attainable but also encouraged. Social media platforms have amplified this phenomenon, creating an environment where people showcase their possessions, vacations, and lifestyles to thousands or even millions of followers. The digital applause from this virtual audience further reinforces the desire to maintain and flaunt a luxurious life, often regardless of whether it is financially sustainable or emotionally fulfilling.

However, like the house built on sand, a life founded on temporary pleasures and material displays can be extremely fragile. Economic downturns, sudden job loss, or global crises can sweep away financial stability in an instant. When this happens, those who have overextended themselves—living paycheck to paycheck to keep up appearances—often find themselves without a safety net. The illusion of permanence disappears, revealing the consequences of not building on a stronger, more enduring foundation.

The parable of the wise and foolish builders is a timeless reminder that life must be anchored in deeper values. While material success and comfort are not wrong in themselves, they should not be the only or primary goals. Building a life on integrity, wisdom, humility, and faith creates a stability that withstands the inevitable storms. In an age where appearance often outweighs substance, it is more crucial than ever to invest in what truly lasts.

99. THE POPULAR PERSONAL PRAYER

Therefore I tell you, whatever you ask in prayer, believe that you have received it, and it will be yours. - Mark 11: 24.

The soul is what sets human beings apart from animals. Unlike animals, humans have the ability to distinguish between right and wrong. This moral awareness is an essential part of human nature, guiding individuals in their decisions and actions. When a person commits a wrongful act, they are often aware of their mistake. However, if they do not acknowledge or repent for their wrongdoing, they may continue repeating the same behavior. Over time, this uncorrected habit can become ingrained in their character and even shape their way of life.

Prayer is a universal practice observed by people across different cultures and religions. Most individuals engage in prayer at least once a day, seeking guidance, strength, and inner peace. While some may pray for material possessions such as wealth, success, or a comfortable home, these requests are relatively rare. The majority of people turn to prayer as a means of seeking spiritual growth and moral purification. They ask for divine help in overcoming their weaknesses and vices, hoping to become better versions of themselves.

Vices, or bad habits, can be deeply ingrained in a person's nature. Some negative traits are so powerful that they persist throughout an individual's life and can even define their legacy. Addictions, dishonesty, laziness, lust, greed, and cruelty are examples of vices that can dominate a person's actions if left unchecked. Without conscious effort to overcome them, these habits may ultimately consume the person, dictating their behavior and choices. It is only through self-awareness and genuine effort that one can begin the process of change.

To free oneself from the grip of vices, certain steps must be taken. The first and most important step is repentance—acknowledging one's wrongdoings and feeling genuine remorse. Along with repentance, fasting can be a powerful tool in developing self-discipline and spiritual clarity (Matthew 6). Acts of kindness, such as helping others in need, also contribute to personal transformation by fostering a sense of humility and compassion. Finally, seeking forgiveness, both from those who have been wronged and from a higher power, is crucial in the journey toward self-improvement.

Overcoming vices is not an easy task, but it is essential for personal and spiritual growth. It requires determination, effort, and the willingness to change. Those who actively work towards self-improvement find themselves living more fulfilling lives, free from the burden of negative habits. Through repentance, prayer, fasting, and acts of kindness, one can gradually transform their character and live a life of virtue. In doing so, they not only uplift themselves but also inspire those around them to strive for goodness and moral excellence.

100. WHAT HAPPENS ON EARTH STAYS ON EARTH

"Repent, for the kingdom of heaven has come near." - Matthew 3:2.

One of the slogans made popular by Las Vegas tourism was: What happens in Vegas stays in Vegas. The idea is simple—you can act however you want while there, and once you leave, it remains behind. Yet, when we reflect spiritually, this phrase takes on a much deeper meaning. What happens on Earth, both good and bad, has consequences, but through God's grace, our sins need not follow us beyond the grave. Instead, they can remain behind if we choose to turn away from them and seek forgiveness.

Life on Earth is filled with temptations, mistakes, and sins. Every human being stumbles, but the message of the Gospel is clear: we are not doomed to carry our failures into eternity. Repentance is the gift that wipes the slate clean. By confessing our wrongs and sincerely turning our hearts back to God, the sins committed here stay here. Heaven is not a place where guilt and shame dwell; it is a place for those who have embraced God's mercy and sought His forgiveness while still on Earth.

The Bible reminds us of a powerful example at the crucifixion of Jesus. Two thieves hung on either side of Him, but only one recognized who He truly was. With humility, the thief on Jesus' right repented, asking to be remembered in the kingdom. Christ's response was immediate and full of compassion: "Today you will be with me in paradise." This is the only man explicitly assured of heaven in Scripture—not because of a life lived without fault, but because of genuine repentance in his final moments.

The same promise is extended to us today. We may carry the weight of many sins, but those burdens do not have to follow us beyond this life. If we repent, believe, and walk in God's mercy, our sins remain on Earth, never to enter heaven with us. That is the hope and assurance of the Gospel—that what happens on Earth can indeed stay on Earth, leaving us free to enter eternity cleansed, forgiven, and made whole through Christ.

101. THE FINAL REQUEST: ENTRUSTING THE LOVED ONE

This is the confidence that we have in our relationship with God: If we ask for anything in agreement with his will, he listens to us. -1 John 5:14.

Once I was walking through Arlington National Cemetery in Virginia, a place of solemn beauty and deep reverence. Spanning more than 600 acres, it serves as the final resting place for countless servicemen and women, along with their families. From its hilltop, the cemetery offers a sweeping panoramic view of Washington, D.C., reminding visitors of the ideals and sacrifices that built and protect the nation.

As I wandered along the winding paths lined with perfectly ordered white headstones, I noticed a little girl, no more than five or six years old, walking just a few steps ahead of me on the edge of the footpath. She had long hair that danced in the gentle breeze, and beside her walked her father, his posture protective yet tender. They were just a few meters ahead, their quiet presence harmonizing with the silence of the grounds.

I was walking at a faster pace and was nearly about to pass them when, suddenly, I heard a clear, firm voice in my mind: "Look at the child."

Instinctively, I resisted. "No," I replied inwardly, "it is rude to stare." At that very moment, the girl stumbled and fell to the ground. Her father bent quickly to lift her, and as she turned her face upward, I saw clearly for the first time— she was a child with Down syndrome.

I continued walking, but my mind lingered on the moment. Why, I wondered, did God be in a cemetery? Then I looked around me and saw families scattered across the grounds, visiting the graves of their loved ones. All of them standing in silence, many lost in memory. Every day, nearly twenty-five new funerals take place at the Arlington Cemetery, each one marking the final chapter of a family's story of love, loss, and remembrance.

In a place so full of grief, one common prayer seems to rise from every heart: "Lord, take care of the soul of the one we loved." The families entrust their loved ones to God. Perhaps that is why God is here—because love, sorrow, memory, trust and hope converge in the sacred ground. In the stillness of Arlington Cemetery, one realizes that God walks alongside the living and the dead, and answering the prayers they entrust him.

The world is neither simply black and white nor merely filled with color; it is far beyond such definitions. Existence does not confine itself to three dimensions—it unfolds in infinite dimensions that stretch beyond the limits of human perception. What we perceive with our senses is only a fraction of reality. There are things visible to the eye, yet countless more remain hidden, existing in realms we cannot measure or fully understand. What appears tangible and real may in fact be virtual, a reflection or an illusion shaped by perspective. The universe had a beginning, and in time, it will also reach its end. Yet within this fleeting cycle lies a deeper truth: while the body is temporary, fragile, and bound by time, the soul is eternal, enduring beyond the boundaries of life and death, carrying with it the essence of who we are.